About the Author

Miriam Fields-Babineau is a professional animal trainer, author of 32 books on animal training and provides animals for media productions. She has trained many Labradoodles and other mixed breeds in her classes over the years. She designed the Comfort Trainer Head Halter, All-in-One Training Leash and other animal training products. She resides on a farm in Virginia with her husband, son and many beloved pets.

About Our Cover Dog

Meet Shayna, a two-year-old Labradoodle, owned by Hally Birnbaum and Doug Heimbigner of New York. Shayna was bred by Nancy Smallwoods of the Doodlesville kennels. Shayna's favorite activity is playing soccer with her two playmates, Coco, a chocolate Labrador Retriever (no relation), and Duffy, a Shepadoodle. Her friends call her "Ms. Personality," as she's in love with everyone. When not sharing the company of her owners and playmates, Shayna enjoys eating cheese, any kind except blue.

Labradoodle

By Miriam Fields-Babineau

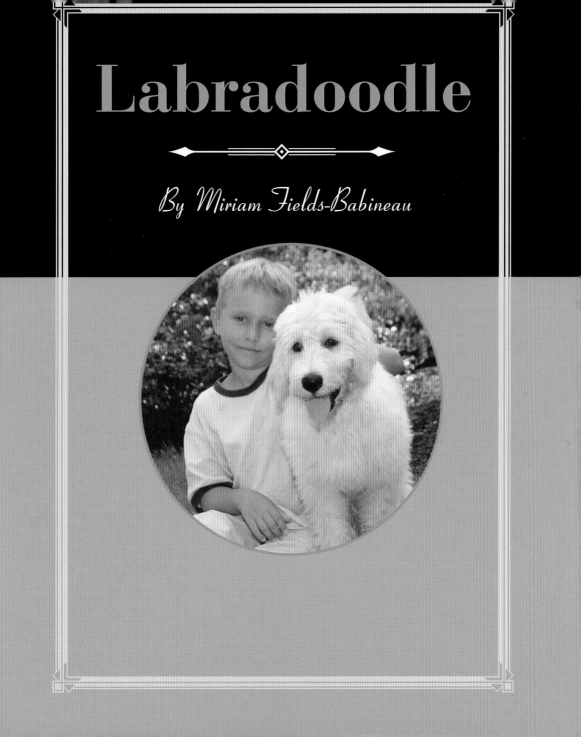

Making a splash in every state in the Union (and every province above), here's the newest Yankee Doodle!

Acknowledgments

Many thanks to all of the fabulous Doodle owners who shared their dogs with our photographer Mary Bloom. These include Hally Birnbaum, the Chesterman family, Mort and Susan Goldstein, Laura Harker, Doug Heimbigner, the Lawler family, Steve and Jane Lifrak, Liz Patterson, the Rist family and Donn Tobin. Special thanks to Mark Daims, DVM.

And here's a shout-out to thoughtful owners who sent in their photos, including Malinda DeVincenzi, Kathleen Rally and Nancy Smallwood.

Kennel Club Books®, the country's only major publisher of exclusively dog books, proudly presents its *Designer Dog Series*™ to celebrate the Labradoodle's coming-out party. Continuing in its bold effort to produce a unique line of dog books, Kennel Club Books® releases the first ever book on the specific designer dog crossbreeds. The company has also released many *Special Limited Editions* and *Special Rare-Breed Editions* on various unusual breeds.

Visit the publisher's website at
www.kennelclubbooks.com
to read more about the unique library of books available to dog lovers around the world.

KENNEL CLUB BOOKS®

Designer Dog
SERIES™

LABRADOODLE
ISBN 13: 978-159378670-0

Copyright © 2006, 2008
Kennel Club Books® a Division of BowTie, Inc.
40 Broad Street, Freehold, NJ 07728 USA
Printed in South Korea

Photography by:
Mary Bloom

with additional photos by
Callea Photo, Isabelle Français
and Carol Ann Johnson.

10 9 8 7 6 5

Contents

Labrador Retriever, yellow.

Miniature Poodle, black.

What do you get when you cross the world's two smartest breeds?

Labradoodle?

Dogs have been domesticated for over 14,000 years. They came into our lives as alarms to warn us of intruders, progressing from there to hunting partners and finally to companions. As canines became domesticated, humans also became more diverse, needing canines to aid them in everything from gathering flocks, pulling carts, fetching meals and aiding the disabled. Each breed was developed to fill specific niches in our cultures and lifestyles. There are currently well over 400 breeds of dog in existence, many recognized by the various kennel clubs around the world. Many breeds are still in their infancy as breeders try to standardize their dogs to fit specific physical and behavioral guidelines.

Labradoodles were first developed in the late 1980s by Wally Conran of Guide Dogs Victoria in Kew, Victoria, Australia as assistance dogs for the physically challenged. Guide Dogs Victoria had been contacted by a blind woman who resided in Hawaii and who suffered from severe allergies. She really wanted a dog to aid her in everyday activities but was leery of obtaining one because of her physical reactions to dander and dog fur. A benefit to obtaining a dog from Australia was that the dog would not have to spend time in quarantine upon landing in Hawaii. As Australia is considered an island with strict quarantine laws, Hawaii allows pets imported from Australia to go directly to their owners' homes with no holding period.

A new contender!

Looking back at the origins of many breeds, we see that they were developed to fill some sort of need or niche for which no breed yet existed. Guide Dogs Victoria filled the need for a non-allergenic guide dog by pairing one of their proven Labrador Retrievers, which had been bred specifically for use as an assistance dog, with a Standard Poodle, a breed known for intelligence, sensitivity and low shedding. Imported from Sweden, the Poodle used in the mating was a white dog from working bloodlines. This mating resulted in three allergen-reduced puppies that fit the requirements of assistance dogs that could be matched with people suffering from allergies. Wally Conran dubbed this first litter "Labradoodles."

A few years later a man who supplies puppies to pet shops started breeding Labradoodles. He bred back in more Poodle and continued further by breeding Labradoodle to Labradoodle. His aim was to breed great family pets, but he didn't recognize that a main asset was the low- or non-shedding coat. He continued breeding these first- and second-generation Labradoodles for a few years but did not keep records.

Guide Dogs Victoria had limited success with their Labradoodles but never achieved consistency in order to turn them into a recognized breed. Other kennels in Australia fell in love with the idea of the Labradoodle and tried to recreate Mr. Conran's results. However, most breedings resulted in inconsistencies, causing many of the puppies to have either the double coat of the Labrador Retriever or the mostly curly single coat of the Poodle. Today, although some standardization has been achieved over the decades, there are still few "breed specifications" for the Labradoodle and, as such, it cannot be considered a registerable breed by the American Kennel Club (AKC).

In the 1980s two breeding and research centers were created to try to generate a

Cute and curly well
describes the
Labradoodle of today.

Parent Possibilities

The Labradoodle Association of Australia, Inc. (LAA) has named the following
six breeds as the only approved parent breeds to be used in Labradoodle
breeding: Labrador Retriever, Poodle, Irish Water Spaniel, Curly-Coated
Retriever, (American) Cocker Spaniel and English Cocker Spaniel. Those
wishing to cross to one of the parent breeds must submit documentation and
meet certain specifications as set forth by the LAA.

consistent outcome for the Labradoodle: Rutland Manor Labradoodle Breeding and Research Center Australia, owned by Beverley Manners, and Tegan Park Labradoodle Breeding and Research Center Australia, owned by Beverley's daughter, Angela Cunningham. These centers started keeping track of parentage and maintaining strict breeding standards of health and physical specifications, attributes necessary for any successful breeding program. Both breeding centers, still in operation, have the desire to create what they see as the perfect pet: a dog that has the sturdiness of a Labrador Retriever and a non-shedding coat, is intelligent, has a great temperament and has a teddy-bear appearance that holds him dear to many hearts.

Beverley Manners of Rutland Manor

Irish Water Spaniel.

has bred up to 8 generations of Labradoodles in the past 15 years. However, there are still problems of unpredictability due to gene dominance issues. As both research centers continue to develop and export Labradoodles around the world, the Labradoodle Association of Australia, Inc. (LAA) was formed to provide breeding guidelines as well as to provide support to those who purchase and produce Labradoodles.

Early in the development of Labradoodles, Tegan Park added Irish Water Spaniel blood into the mix to create the dark chocolate coat seen today in many dogs. This addition is called a "parent breeding." There are many Labradoodles that carry the name "Irish" in

Newfoundland.

their registrations. One such example is Tegan Park's Irish Night, who has a direct trace back to the Irish Water Spaniel.

Also added to the Labradoodle mixture was the Curly-Coated Retriever. This crossing produced the more open face, meaning shorter hair on the face than on the body. The only drawback was the aloofness common to the Curly-Coated Retriever breed. Since this crossing, the aloofness has been successfully bred out of the Labradoodle.

Between seven and ten years ago, Tegan Park and Rutland Manor decided to add miniatures to their lines. They originally used Miniature Poodles, which made the resulting Labradoodles lighter in frame. This was not a desired quality, so they brought in both American and English Cocker Spaniels. This produced a dog of soft, silky hair and a stockier body type. It also brought in a domed head and long ears, both of which were not desired. Currently, breeders are selecting dogs without these qualities as breeding stock.

MEET THE PARENTS
You may be thinking, "Why would anyone take two pure-bred dogs, these in particular, perfectly suited for their occupations, and breed them together?" To answer this question, you should first consider the origins of these pure breeds. What's really interesting is that Labrador Retrievers were originally developed from crosses between Newfoundlands, French Poodles and water spaniels. Poodles are already in their background. Is the Labradoodle a step back in the history of the Labrador Retriever?

The first retriever-type dog, known specifically for his abilities to retrieve downed fowl in both the field and water, was the small Newfoundland. This breed didn't actually begin in Newfoundland, a place that had first been inhabited by the

Curly-Coated Retriever.

Dorset Eskimos, who incidentally had no dogs. After Newfoundland was discovered by Bristol traders in 1494, the area became a huge exporter of salted fish. European fishermen brought their own dogs and utilized them for fetching fish that escaped the nets. Through generations of selective breeding, the Newfoundland breed was developed as the perfect dog for this job.

Early in the breed's development, the soft mouths ("soft" meaning having the ability to carry things, like game, in their mouths without damaging them) of these canines proved invaluable, as they were also utilized to supplement their owners' food sources. As English gentry became embroiled in the organized shooting of pheasant, grouse and partridge, they gained interest in the retrieving dog of Newfoundland. They preferred the short, water-resistant coat, otter-shaped tail and ability to withstand cool temperatures. The retrieving dog soon replaced pointers and setters as the dog of choice for this sport. Another great attribute was the retrieving dog's disposition. He was easily trained, amiable and intelligent. He not only performed well in the field but also fit in well with the family.

As the English gentry utilized their retrieving dogs, many began to cross-breed them with French Poodles and water spaniels to increase specific characteristics. These crossings made the retriever a better swimmer, gave him the ability to flush birds as well as retrieve them and increased both his intelligence and stamina. Through the years, specific characteristics were stabilized, and the retrievers developed into the most sought-after hunting companions.

The first retriever ever to be recognized by the American Kennel Club was the Curly-Coated Retriever. This breed was totally suited as a hunting dog, offering keen sensitivity and the desire to perform. The breed's coat was close to water-proof, hardly shed at all and required little grooming

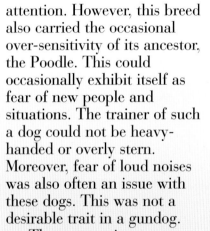

A colorful beginning: the three acceptable colors of the Labrador Retriever, black, yellow and chocolate.

attention. However, this breed also carried the occasional over-sensitivity of its ancestor, the Poodle. This could occasionally exhibit itself as fear of new people and situations. The trainer of such a dog could not be heavy-handed or overly stern. Moreover, fear of loud noises was also often an issue with these dogs. This was not a desirable trait in a gundog.

The next retriever recognized by the AKC was the Flat-Coated Retriever. This breed had all of the attributes required to be a good hunting companion, but it still had the long coat that could get caught up in briers or build up ice when hunting in the snow or cold weather, thus hampering the dog's performance.

The Labrador Retriever was the next retriever recognized. It had been recognized by The Kennel Club of England in July of 1903 and has since become the favored breed for hunting waterfowl. With its short water-resistant coat, strong otter-shaped tail that aids in speedy water retrieval, high prey drive and pleasant nature as a pet, the Labrador Retriever has become the number-one breed in popularity, both as a pet and as a hunting companion. At present, the Labrador is ranked first in popularity according to American Kennel Club registration statistics.

The breed characteristics of the Labrador Retriever are as follows: the height at the shoulder for males is 22.5 to 24.5 inches; females are 21.5 to 23.5 inches. The average weight is 55 to 80 pounds, from the smaller females to the larger males, and the coat is straight, thick and close. The head is broad and well domed, leaving a wide brainpan. The ears are set rather far back and fairly high, folded over. The muzzle should tend to be square, not sharp, which aids in the necessary soft mouth. With a broad chest, laid-back shoulders, well-sprung ribs and a straight back, the Labrador Retriever is athletic and strong. The breed is seen in three colors: black, which is all-black, yellow and chocolate, the latter two permitting some range in the shade.

The Poodle is also a very popular breed and in this age of designer dogs is being mixed with everything from retrievers to schnauzers to spaniels to toy breeds. The intended outcome is a dog that doesn't shed or aggravate people's allergies. These breedings can also provide a dog that is intelligent, social and family-oriented. While the Labradoodle is currently the most popular Poodle mix, the Cockapoo (Cocker Spaniel/Poodle) has been around for decades, as has the Schnoodle (schnauzer/ Poodle), Yorkipoo (Yorkshire Terrier/Poodle) and Peekapoo (Pekingese/Poodle). Adding the Poodle to the mix enhances specific attributes that phase out terrier-like tenacity and other assertive qualities while reducing the incidence of dander and shedding.

Why is the Poodle the dog of choice? Why not the Portuguese Water Dog? These two breeds have similar coats that offer anti-allergic reactions and virtually no shedding. The Bichon Frise is another dog with a curly non-shedding coat. However, it is not just the Poodle's coat that offers enhanced attributes in its progeny: it is also the breed's temperament and behavioral tendencies. Poodles are intelligent, work-driven and loyal. They are eager to learn. They are one of the oldest breeds known to modern man, having been used as hunting partners to retrieve waterfowl, as they are spectacular swimmers.

Poodles first appeared on Greek and Roman coins as well as on Roman tombs as early as

The Labrador Retriever is the most popular companion dog in America, and for many good reasons. This Labradoodle pup knows that it's fun to have a famous mom.

30 AD. In the 16th century the breed as we know it today appeared in Germany and western Russia. It was known as the "Pudel," or "Puddeln," meaning "puddle dog," a dog that likes splashing in water. It was during this time that the Poodle was used primarily as a hunting dog, especially for waterfowl.

In many parts of Europe, the Poodle became a popular working dog, offering assistance to farmers and laborers. In France the breed became so popular that it became the national dog, hence becoming called the French Poodle. A favorite French expression is translated to "loyal as a Poodle."

In the 17th century Poodles became known in England, where they were used primarily as water retrievers. It is unknown whether the Poodle was a descendant of the water dogs or vice versa. However, they are closely related.

Around 1700 the French discovered the Poodle's natural abilities as a performer, and the breed began to be included in the performing arts, making the Poodle popular throughout all of Europe. Poodles still perform in circuses today. In the late 1800s Poodles came to the United States, earning recognition with the American Kennel Club in 1887. For decades the Poodle has remained on America's top-ten list of popular dogs, having enjoyed the number-one position many times.

Poodles have an average lifespan of 12 years, with the

Nosy, fun and hypoallergenic, too! Three cheers for Poodles!

Miniature and Toy varieties sometimes living to 16 or more years. They are seen in a wide variety of solid colors, from white to black and almost everything in between. Their coats are dense and curly with a harsh texture. Poodles require frequent grooming and clipping to maintain cleanliness, which is not a preferred trait in a hunting dog, thus their popularity as hunting partners diminished but they have become very desirable companion dogs. Due to the breed's folded, or drop, ear, it can be prone to ear infections; therefore the ears should be checked and cleaned as often as twice a week. The smaller varieties can also have dental problems. Toothbrushing is suggested at least every other day, with regular veterinary dental checks.

We've mentioned that while the Poodle's history as an excellent working dog and the lack of shedding, odor and dander make the breed a very appealing one to use in cross-breeding, the breed's behavioral qualities offer even more advantages. The Poodle is mild-mannered, yet protective of his home. He is good with children. The Poodle is highly intelligent, with excellent problem-solving abilities. What more could a person want? He is precise in his responses, with a great sense of routine and timing.

Now that we've explored the backgrounds of both breeds, you can see why the combination of Labrador Retriever and Poodle is an attractive one. Pairing the two breeds offers a non-allergenic, intelligent dog that is good with people of all ages, loves to work and has the stamina, ability and desire to aid the disabled, and do so in a precise manner. A Labradoodle can be a fabulous dog, provided he is in a loving home that offers appropriate care, training and exercise. This "breed" requires daily exercise and will not do well if not given the opportunity for some daily free-running time in a place like a safely fenced yard or off-leash dog run. This book will guide you in how to provide your fantastic Labradoodle with all he needs to live as a healthy, happy, productive companion.

The best of all possible worlds...

Doodle Nature of the
Labradoodle

Combining a Labrador

Retriever with a Poodle does not do much to change the intrinsic nature of the outcome. Both breeds are intelligent, eager to please, loyal and hard-working with high energy levels and the ability to learn quickly. However, the Labrador Retriever tends to be more outgoing than the Poodle, which can sometimes be aloof. The main differences in the progeny are the coat and a slightly higher sensitivity to the environment without being overly fearful.

Labradoodles are great with children, although they may be a little too much for very young children, as they are high-energy dogs. A young child can accidentally be hurt if he is unintentionally bumped or pushed over by a playful Labradoodle. Older children do well with Labradoodles because the dogs are happy to romp and play for long periods of time. They don't mind a slight amount of rough-and-tumble, nor do they get mouthy or pushy. In fact, the author has never heard about a Labradoodle that has shown any aggressive tendencies, even when frightened.

Labradoodles are also very social. They easily accept other dogs and new people. In fact, they welcome newcomers into the pack with delight. Although they may bark when a stranger is near their territory, they will not go beyond that into any type of "attack mode." As soon as they have a chance to sniff the stranger, that

the Labradoodle has it all.

person or animal is welcomed. A Labradoodle can't be counted on to protect the home and family unless the intruder is intimidated by the size and sound of the canine; otherwise, it is likely that he will be cajoled into a game and licked all over.

What is most important about Labradoodles is their intelligence. It is equal to that of a Border Collie or Australian Shepherd, regarded as among the most intelligent breeds, but without the constant "eye" to work and over-sensitivity to emotion. Labradoodles like to be directed. Having been shown how to do something once or twice, they have a full understanding and delight in performing the task. To them it's not a drive to perform, it's an enjoyment of activity. These qualities make them perfect assistance dogs. Their abilities to reason through complex circumstances are remarkable.

Due to these characteristics, Labradoodles have the tendency to outfox their owners if not trained and guided properly. This is typical of any intelligent animal that learns how to

obtain what he wants. A Labradoodle will display a behavior and, if rewarded in some manner, will continue to perform this behavior. Labradoodle owners must train their dogs! Training brings harmony. The dog will thus learn proper guidelines, happily abiding by them.

Physically, Labradoodles can withstand very extreme temperatures, both hot and cold. Their coats will protect them against both extremes. The retriever blood gives the dog a love of romping in the snow or an icy lake. The Poodle blood gives the dog a love of romping in any weather, just as long as he can romp. Both breeds have water-resistant coats and adore swimming. In fact, it's tough to keep a Labradoodle out of water!

Along with their energy and love of activity, Labradoodles also like to rest at their owners' feet. They love to be touching their human companions. They readily partake in anything, provided it is with their families, to which they are very loyal.

Whether it's a duck, quail or squeaky toy, your Labradoodle will be happy to show off his retriever prowess.

In many breeds a specific sex might be preferred for certain characteristics. For example, many female dogs tend to be easier to train, while male dogs might be more territorial. Labradoodles don't tend to have sex-specific temperament traits. Labradoodles were created to be all-around loving, loyal family dogs as well as extremely good service dogs. Males and females alike are terrific at both.

Keeping in mind the Labradoodle's behavior characteristics, we must consider who would be ideal Labradoodle owners. As great as a Labradoodle is as a pet, this isn't a dog for everyone.

An active, loving family with a
priceless new addition....another
blond sibling joins the pack.

IDEAL FAMILY

- Is active;
- Takes the time to train and stimulate their dog;
- Continually offers positive reinforcement and new stimuli in the environment;
- Spends a lot of time with their dog;
- Gives the dog time to play with other dogs;
- Maintains a regular daily routine and schedule;
- Has no children or has well-behaved school-aged children.

NON-IDEAL FAMILY

- Is very sedate when home;
- Is looking for an independent, couch-potato-type dog;
- Travels for both business and pleasure to destinations inappropriate for dogs;
- Does not have a regular daily routine or schedule;
- Does not usually encounter situations that allow for the dog to interact with other dogs;
- Has little or no experience with an active breed and the training required for a dog;
- Has very young children (under five years of age).

Schedule-Oriented

Labradoodles thrive on routine, knowing what will happen and when. Without this, they might develop neuroses, for their lives will be inconsistent. Inconsistency breeds insecurity. Things like maintaining specific feeding and exercise times will help your Labradoodle live in a more relaxed manner.

Family outings can be fun for all, but both kids and Doodles must be well behaved.

A FAMILY AFFAIR

An active family that has time to include their dog in their daily routines will provide a perfect home for a Labradoodle. Belonging to someone who needs an assistance dog is also a great situation for this breed, as the dog will constantly be working and accompanying his person everywhere. A human companion who involves his dog in organized canine sports and activities, such as agility, flyball, freestyle and hunting events will be good for a Labradoodle as well.

This is not a dog that should be locked up for long hours. Labradoodles have supreme intelligence and high energy levels. Labradoodles need people who want to train them and spend significant amounts of time with them. They are inquisitive and energetic. These qualities can get them into trouble if left home alone for long hours without adequate exercise. A "latch key" Labradoodle is likely to become destructive and develop separation anxiety. Being crated or penned

The intelligent Doodle excels in training classes with his owner.

excessively will be frustrating for a Labradoodle, so the family must have a dog-proof room or area of the house where the dog can stay when alone, with no danger of causing himself harm or getting into trouble. A happily active Labradoodle, though, is one that should be content to rest and relax when left home alone.

Training is the key to avoiding a dog with behavioral issues when left alone. A trained Labradoodle is safe when left home alone for reasonable periods of time. Labradoodles have a good idea of what constitutes desired behavior. However, this only works when they learn by their desired behavior's being rewarded. If not rewarded, they will partake in undesirable behavior because that still earns them attention, even if it's not positive attention. Labradoodles are attention hogs. They will quickly learn how to attain attention of any type. It is up to you, the Labradoodle owner, to guide your dog in the right direction. Don't sit and complain—train and explain!

Designed for helping mankind, not for fashion...

Developing the
Labradoodle

Labradoodles have been around

for over three decades, but there has not yet been any real type of standardization of the "breed." This is due not only to the complications of genetics but also to the fact that many breeders have not restricted their own breeding practices. Labradoodles have become very popular very quickly. Hence, breeders have popped up everywhere with few restrictions on or expectations of what they produce.

Remember that Labradoodles were originally created as service dogs. The best size for a service dog is medium to large. A small dog cannot possibly manage to physically aid a handicapped person, other than by alerting, signaling or fetching small items. A larger dog can pull someone along or allow himself to be used to help someone up. Thus Standard Poodles were used along with the Labrador Retriever in the original Labradoodle breedings. However, this made for a very large dog, too large to be manageable for the physically disabled.

The Tegan Park and Rutland Manor Breeding Centers began trying to standardize the Labradoodle into two sizes, medium and miniature. The medium Labradoodle is suited to aiding the physically disabled, while the miniature variety is suited to working as seizure-alerting dogs or to assisting the elderly and hearing impaired. The miniatures are also successful as therapy dogs. To a person apprehen-

here's a Doodle at your service.

A miniature Labradoodle, showing how tall he really feels!

SIZE DIFFERENCES
There are four sizes of Poodle: Standard, Miniature, Toy and Teacup, although the Teacup is not recognized by the AKC or the Poodle Club of America. The Labrador Retriever is seen in only one size. Mixing the Labrador with the various sizes of Poodle does little to help with standardizing the size of the Labradoodle.

sive of dogs, their smaller size is less threatening than that of a larger-sized dog.

In order for any breed to be recognized as a pure breed, certain parameters have to be met. First of all, there has to be a specific number of dogs within the country in which recognition is being sought. For the American Kennel Club, this number is 300 in at least 20 states. The AKC also requires there to be a national breed club that demonstrates sufficient interest and offers breeder/owner support. Additionally, there must be a recorded three-generation pedigree, meaning one that proves only Labradoodle-to-Labradoodle pairings for at least three generations.

Not only must there be an apparent interest in promoting the breed but the dogs also must have predictable characteristics that fulfill a specific purpose. The two breeds that form the Labradoodle come from two different groups. Groups are clusters of breeds designated by the kennel clubs in which dogs of similar type and/or purpose are classified. With the AKC, the

Labrador Retriever is in the Sporting Group and the Standard Poodle is in the Non-Sporting Group, as the Poodle today has a more general companion nature rather than a specific working purpose. Even today the Poodle is sometimes used as a hunting partner and was used as a hunting dog long before the Labrador Retriever was developed, but Poodles are not popular today as hunting dogs because of certain physical attributes. A Labradoodle might perform well as a hunting dog, but his coat is not of desirable type for a dog used in the field, as it will tend to become entangled in brush. Labrador Retrievers are stronger swimmers and can work better in cooler environments for longer.

Picture this: a camouflaged hunter strolling through the marshes with a...Poodle? I doubt many hunters would be caught in the fields, never mind attending field trials, with their Poodles. Call it a "macho" attitude if you like. The Labrador Retriever is still the dog of choice for waterfowl hunting.

GUARDING THE BREED

The Labradoodle Association of Australia, Inc. was formed by breeders who wished to guard this developing breed and create a common goal: "An all-around great dog that is non-shedding and allergy friendly." This statement comes from the Labradoodle Association of Australia's website, www.laa.org.au.

A great example of an all-around terrific designer dog.

Dense, thick and non-shedding, a coat of many colors, from chalk to black, is seen in the Labradoodle.

PHYSICAL AND HEALTH CHARACTERISTICS OF THE LABRADOODLE

If a Labrador Retriever is bred with a Standard Poodle, the result will be pups that grow up to be anywhere from 21 to 24 inches at the shoulder. A female might weigh from 45 to 60 pounds, while a male will weigh as much as 55 to 80 pounds. If the Lab is bred with a large Miniature Poodle, the Labradoodle will stand approximately 18 to 22 inches at the shoulder and weigh from 40 to 55 pounds. If the Labradoodle had been bred from crossing a smaller Miniature Poodle with a Labrador, the height might be anywhere from 14 to 20 inches at the shoulder and weight could range from 26 to 55 pounds.

There are three types of coat possibilities for Labradoodles; all are easy to maintain, but not all are allergy-friendly. First, the "hair coat" can range from flat to straight, wavy or curly. This type of coat also can range from being slick like the coat of a Labrador, to having feathering on the tail, legs and face, to wavy all over. This coat sheds in varying degrees and is not the desirable coat type for the Labradoodle. The second type is the "fleece coat," which is like that of an angora goat. This type of coat is a single coat, soft and curly and should not shed. Finally, the "woolly coat" is much like the coat of a pure-bred Poodle, offering a non-shedding dog. The coat is dense and thick, sometimes a dense plush with curls that aren't as tight as on a Poodle. A Labradoodle with either the fleece or woolly coat is the dog of choice for allergy sufferers, and these are the types to which we are referring when we mention the non-allergenic, non-shedding coat.

The coat length should be anywhere from 4 to 6 inches, with colors that include cream, chalk, apricot, black, silver, blue, chocolate, coffee, red, gold and café-au-lait. Most Labradoodles are either black

The silver lining at one end of the Doodle rainbow.

or golden tan, as these are the most dominant color genes.

In general appearance, the Labradoodle is slightly heavier than a Standard Poodle, though not as robust as a Labrador Retriever. The Labradoodle's forelimbs are muscular. The ears lie flat against the head and are set level with the eye. The ear leather is of medium thickness, and the ear doesn't hang lower than the lip line. The head should be broad, chiseled and clean. The Labradoodle's eyes are round, expressive and set well apart. Like that of the retriever, the Labradoodle's nose is large, square and fleshy. A preferred tail set is low and saber-like, although a high-set tail is acceptable.

Labradoodle life expectancy is somewhere between that of the Poodle, at 12 to 18 years, and that of the Labrador Retriever, at 12 to 14 years. Many Labradoodle breeders have determined their dogs' average lifespans to be 13 to 15 years.

Poorly bred dogs might be prone to certain genetic defects that are common in pure-breds: hip dysplasia, von Willebrand's disease (a blood-clotting disorder), progressive retinal atrophy (which causes blindness), elbow problems and patellar disorders. If the dogs to be bred show no signs of these defects at least three generations back in their pedigrees, there's a good chance that the progeny will be clear of them. When choosing a breeder, be sure to check the pedigrees and health certificates of the parents for three generations. However, it's not unheard of for a puppy to show up with a latent genetic defect from time to time. It's tough to find any Labrador Retriever with a clear genetic record that goes back three generations. The Labrador has been a popular breed for a long time, which makes for unscrupulous breeders who breed only to meet the demand and are not conscientious about what they produce. If your Labradoodle breeder has records for at least three generations, it's a pretty safe bet that you've met a good breeder.

A good Labradoodle

breeder will also have both parents examined and hips x-rayed for genetic faults. A Labrador Retriever should not be bred without a certification number for healthy hips from the Orthopedic Foundation for Animals (OFA) or another accredited organization (testing schemes vary from country to country), or without a clearance for progressive retinal atrophy (PRA), along with three generations of clear parentage. The Poodle should also be tested as clear of PRA, von Willebrand's disease, skin disorders and hip dysplasia. The Poodle's hip scores should be excellent in order to counter the Labrador Retriever's tendency to have dysplasia issues.

Different Types of Crosses

The F_1 line is what is known as the first line of parentage and in the Labradoodle refers to the pairing of a Labrador Retriever and a Poodle. An F_1B mating is an F_1 Labradoodle back-crossed to a pure-bred Poodle. A multi-generational mating is Labradoodle to Labradoodle; to ensure good health, unrelated Labradoodles should be used in this type of mating. Likewise, with the F_1B, the Labradoodle and Poodle should be unrelated. This is called "out-crossing," where "line-breeding" is when dogs of the same bloodline are mated together.

BREEDING ISSUES

In October of 2004, the Labradoodle Association of Australia, Inc. set up the Breed Infusion Committee to set forth rules for using parent breeds in Labradoodle breeding. In addition to the Poodle and the Labrador Retriever, the following breeds used in the development of the Labradoodle are approved as parent breeds in Australia: the Irish Water Spaniel, Curly-Coated Retreiver, Cocker Spaniel and English Cocker Spaniel. The rules for using a parent breed in Labradoodle breeding in Australia include the following:

- A passing hip score; with the OFA this is a grade of Fair or better and with the British Veterinary Association this is a score of less than 16;
- Pertinent breed information, such as the pedigree;
- Photographs of the parent breed dog taken from front and side views;
- A notarized statement of good temperament;
- An essay outlining the reasons for the parent breed infusion, to include informa-

tion about the dog's body type and personality;
- Proof of a permanent form of identification such as a tattoo or microchip;
- A DNA profile submitted to the Labradoodle DNA center in Australia.

Some breeders continually cross the Labrador Retriever with a Poodle to obtain their F_1 lines (F_1 referring to first line of parentage) of Labradoodles, while others are confident to cross Labradoodle with Labradoodle (PAL_1 lines) in order to attempt to create a breed standard. Sometimes, after several generations, a pure-bred Poodle will be added back in to correct the coat or disposition. Labradoodle breeders have begun using the terms "multi-gen," "early-gen" and "back-cross." These terms are explained by Melinda Radus:

"A multi-gen Australian Labradoodle is a dog that has had many years in its development and the selection of its foundation stock. It is not fully known today exactly what 'special ingredients' and 'percentages for the parent breeds' are in the multi-gen Australian Labradoodle.

"An early-gen is a dog from new bloodlines that has not had the multiple generations of Labradoodle-to-Labradoodle breeding nor the addition of the Australian Labradoodle foundation stock. These dogs are usually Labrador to Poodle matings and have more tendencies to a shedding coat as they are closer to the genetics of the Labrador Retriever's shedding coat.

"A back-cross refers to when a Labradoodle has to be bred back to one of the parent breeds (usually a Poodle, but this is not restricted). Different breeders do back-crosses for different reasons; some will do back-crosses to correct a coat type, to establish a color or to bring in new bloodlines for their Australian Labradoodles."

As you can see, there are not the consistent outcomes as would be found when breeding pure-breds. When pure-breds are bred together,

A trio of Australian-type Labradoodle pups.

the outcome is a known factor. Although there are allowable variations as well as occasional defects, for the most part size, conformation, disposition, health issues and coloring are known factors. Although more than three

The Poodle dates back to the 12th century, and the Labrador to the 19th century. What took so long to dream me up?

The Allure of Designer Dogs

Poodle mixes are quickly gaining in popularity, even though many pure-bred dog breeders continue to "poo-poo" the Poodle crosses. Nevertheless, the allure of the designer dog has captivated thousands of people, and fortunately there are many dedicated breeders producing healthy, sound and lovely Labradoodles to meet the demand for these undeniably terrific dogs.

Each puppy is unique and offers the benefits of the Poodle heritage: intelligence, an easy-care coat and a nice temperament. The more that people seek out these mixes, the more that breeders will produce them. One must watch out for poorly bred pups, though, as unscrupulous breeders will eagerly mix their breeding stock to fulfill the high demand. The designer-dog purchaser needs to be just as careful when purchasing his Poodle cross as he would be if purchasing a pure-bred.

generations of Labradoodles have been crossed, it is still a breed in development.

As with pure-bred dogs, Labradoodle breeding practices should be confined to those who have a full understanding of the procedures. To avoid genetic inbreeding, a breeder must research the dogs' ancestries. To avoid genetic defects, many physical and health tests must be performed. To avoid other health risks, the dam and the pups must be inoculated, fed and cared for properly. Breeding is not a means of making a living. It is a labor of love. It is a difficult process that requires much study and dedication, a means of developing puppies that will improve a breed or fill a niche in our society. As we've explained, the Labradoodle has arrived to fill a niche—an assistance dog that is easy on the allergy sufferer. At the same time, he also is an intelligent, active and loving dog that is very family-friendly.

Cute, very smart and highly trainable. Did we mention "cute"?

The essence of Labradoodles is ineffable..

The Labradoodle
Breed Standard

We've been careful so far to not call this designer dog a "breed." For all intents and purposes, the Labradoodle in the United States is not a breed. As defined by our eyebrow-raising friends at the American Kennel Club, a breed is "a domestic race of dogs…" (we're okay so far) "…selected and maintained by humans…" (yes, we Doodle lovers are human, and we have selected our dogs) "…with a common gene pool…" ("common"? Doodles are anything but common) "…and a *characterized appearance* and function." By the end of that definition, the Labradoodle falls a few hundred yards short.

The Labradoodle, by definition, is a crossbreed: a combination of two of the most popular dogs on the planet. Few would argue that the Labrador Retriever is a true pure-bred dog, as is the Poodle, yet even these long-established breeds are not without variation. Lab folk don't agree on their own breed standard, and most show dogs don't even come close to that description of the ideal dog. Forget about the pet dogs: they can range from a rangy "field-type" 60-pound dog to a piggy-bank-shaped 120-pounder. In Poodles, type varies somewhat less, unless you go overseas or into some commercial establishments that fake pedigrees and promote 1-pound saucer-fitting dogs. Let's not even mention those forbidden (though terrific) parti-color Poodles!

poetry in motion and prose in reverse.

And from these two breeds, we're going to cross them and get a "characterized appearance"? Not very easily, that's for certain. In Australia, we'll see that the Labradoodle has become more standardized as a "breed" in that breeders are promoting fifth- and sixth-generation litters (Doodle-to-Doodle matings). In the US, crossbreeding of the two parent breeds is more common (although there are breeders with multi-generational lines), and the type, as seen in our handsome models, varies considerably. Nonetheless, the International Labradoodle Association (ILA) of the US has devised a standard for the dog, which is helpful in its detailed description. The Labradoodle Association of Australia also has a standard to which breeders strive to aspire.

The Labradoodle is a crossbreed, but this sociable charmer would never be called cross!

THE INTERNATIONAL LABRADOODLE ASSOCIATION STANDARD FOR THE LABRADOODLE

General Appearance: The Labradoodle comes in three sizes, Standard (largest), Medium (somewhere between the Standard and Miniature size) and Miniature (smallest). There should be no appreciable difference in the general appearance in any of the three sizes.

A compact dog, not exceptionally boxy nor long bodied. A galloping dog which gives the impression of light-footed athleticism, and joyful bearing. Medium to light boning, graceful in movement and with vivacious expression. Coat should be non-shedding, be of even length over body, on legs, neck, tail and head, and should be as close to non-allergenic as possible. Their unique traits of intuitive nature and the seeking of human eye contact should be easily discernible at a glance. Easily amenable to training.

Sizes: The Standard Labradoodle is over 20 inches at the highest point of the shoulders; the Medium Labradoodle is 17 inches to 20 inches to the shoulder; and the Miniature Labradoodle, "Mini," is below 17 inches to above 14 inches at the highest point of the shoulders.

Temperament: Confident, joyful, vivacious, clown-like, sociable and friendly, totally non-aggressive, clever and extremely intuitive. Well suited for special work such as Therapy Dog, Assistance Dog, Hearing or Seizure Alert Dog,

Keeping Records

You may think that recording each pup's time of birth is silly, but you would be surprised at how many people want to run horoscopes on their puppies.

Guide Dog. Can try to outsmart their owners just for fun, if not firmly disciplined when young. Respond well to positive training methods. Loyal and devoted to family. Most love water and are natural swimmers and retrievers. Affectionate and loving. Active and athletic when free, but should "melt" into mellowness when touched by human hands.

Disqualifying Faults: Timidity, hyperactivity, aggressiveness to either people or other animals are all serious disqualifying faults and dogs exhibiting these traits should not be bred from.

Movement: First impression should be of a dog whose feet seem to hardly touch the ground. Light, lithe, graceful, athletic. When trotting, should have the appearance of "going somewhere" with energy and effortless drive and purpose. Looking like they are dancing. When galloping, they should appear to float almost above the ground. Light and airy, flowing and free moving with a complete absence of apparent effort.

Body: Height to length ratio should be as 10 is to 12, being slightly longer in leg than deep in body, but still looking compact. Level topline, strong over loins and slightly sloping croup and with sloping shoulders flowing into firm elbows and front legs straight to the ground. Straight upright shoulders are a fault as are straight stifles. Stifles should have medium angulation and be long, with short strong hocks parallel and straight to the ground. Cow hocks are a fault as are toes turning either inwards or outwards. They are a galloping dog, so flanks should rise to a medium tuck-up, from deep brisket and well-sprung ribs.

Head: The head should be in proportion to the rest of the body, being neither blocky, nor too fine or chiseled. Medium stop, length from nose to eyes should be slightly longer than length from eyes to occiput. Skull should be slightly rounded but not domed. Forehead medium breadth, muzzle not snipey, but should have depth and breadth. Weak

A Medium Labradoodle of Australian type in a silver curly coat.

A Standard Labradoodle in a chocolate wavy coat.

under jaw should be penalized. The head should flow naturally into a strong slightly curved and muscular neck and not appear to be "stuck on." Long narrow head is a fault.

Ears: Should be wide apart and low set, below or level with the eyes and hanging flat against the sides of the head. The inner ear canal should not be too heavily coated. Ear "leather" should be thinner rather than thick and spongy.

Eyes: Should be wide set, large and expressive, lustrous or sparkling, oval to round, and must not bulge (as in the Pekingese for example).

Expression to be lively, curious, full of fun and intuitive-looking, seeking human eye contact. Eye colors can be darkest brown, a transparent honey color or shades of hazel. Wall or china eyes are not permissible. Protruding eyes, sunken or watery eyes are a fault (note that puppies may sometimes have tear-stained eyes during teething).

Nose: Large, square and fleshy in appearance. Must never be narrow or pointed. Brown colored dogs must have "rose" or "liver" colored noses and can never be black. Reds must have black noses. Other colors may have any of the above, depending on the colors they themselves carry in their ancestry.

Teeth: Scissor bite, meaning that the upper teeth fit closely over the tops of the lower teeth. Gaps between upper and lower teeth are a fault. Undershot mouths (where the lower teeth extend beyond the upper teeth) are a fault. Overshot mouths (where the upper teeth extend beyond the lower teeth) are a fault. Crowded teeth in the adult dog are a fault especially in Miniatures.

Tail: Ideally saber shaped as in the Labrador Retriever. But during the formative years of the breed the tail may be carried gaily and swirling over the back. Tightly curled teapot tails are not permissible. Kinked tails are not permissible. White-tipped tails are not permissible. Tails must not be docked.

Feet: Foot pads should be thick and deep and close together. Weak "hare's feet" are a fault. There should be a definite "ankle" between the feet and legs. Front dewclaws may be removed although it is not necessary. It is rare for a Labradoodle to have hind dewclaws but if puppies are born with them, they must be removed at four days old.

Pigment: Must be strong in all colors. Browns must have liver or rose pigment. Apricots and Reds must have black pigment. Missing pigment around the eyes, or spots or patches of white or pink on the nose, eye rims, lips or pads are not permissible.

Coat: As the Labradoodle develops through the generations there are many coat types from short sparse hairy coats, to long flowing hair coats, to woolly curly coats. But the ideal is the non-shedding Fleece or Wool Curly Coat, which must not shed, is allergy-friendly to the vast majority of persons with dog-related allergies and which has no doggy odor. The coat is one of the unique features of this breed and must be a priority coming close behind health and sound temperament.

The Fleece Coat: Fleece coats have a distinctly soft fleecy "feel" like no other dog coat. It should be a single coat, with a complete absence of fluffy undercoat. Ideally it should not be too thick, nor fuzzy, but should hang in loose loopy spirals similar to that of the angora goat. Length is around four to six inches, on body, tail, head and face and on the legs. A "change" of coat is permissible from puppy to adult and due to hormonal changes in entire females. This should not shed itself out, but needs to be stripped out with grooming.

The Wool Curly Coat: The Wool Curly Coat feels similar to that of a pure-bred Poodle and will often be quite tightly curled. But it should be the breeders' goal to breed a looser curl than that of the Poodle in the interest of lower maintenance.

The Hair Coat: Hair Coats can be wavy or curly, short or long and although not ideal, are permissible during the early years of development in breeding programs. If these dogs are exceptional in conformation, temperament and health, they can be valuable breeding dogs when mated to suitable partners and should not be discarded for breeding.

Colors: The Labradoodle coat colors are black, blue, silver, chalk, cream, cafe-au-lait, apricot, red, gold and chocolate. Small white patches as found in the Lab and Poodle at chest and toes are accepted. Accepted color variations include:

Solid: Coat color is solid and even. Clear colors are preferred but natural variations in the shading of the coat are not to be considered a fault.

Parti-colored: At least fifty percent white, with spots or patches of any other acceptable solid color. The head can be of a solid color but white muzzle, blaze or white muzzle/blaze combination (preferably symmetrical) are equally acceptable. Full or partial saddles are acceptable, as long as they do not exceed the color proportion, but are not preferred. Ticking in the white of the coat is acceptable but not preferred.

A young Standard Labradoodle, showing off his swirling tail.

Note: The ILA will accept the registration of any other multi-colored Labradoodle provided DNA testing verifies the parentage.

Serious Faults: Hyperactivity, shyness, timidity, aggressive to people or other animals, snappy, yappy, high-strung, missing pigment, overshot, undershot or crowded mouths, patched color, kinked or teapot tails, weak or "hare" feet, heavy or ponderous build, cow hocks, dippy backs.

Footnote: In these early years of the development of the Labradoodle, it should be the goal of every serious breeder to do their best to safeguard the health status of the Labradoodle for future generations. Testing for hereditary unsoundness in breeding stock will go a long way towards this goal, and although it is no guarantee of the health of their progeny, it should be accepted practice by every breeder to health-test their dogs.

Shortly after her trip to the groomer's, here's Shayna smiling for the camera.

LABRADOODLE ASSOCIATION OF AUSTRALIA—BREED STANDARD OF THE AUSTRALIAN LABRADOODLE 2004

General Appearance: Should be athletic and graceful yet compact with substance and medium boning. Joyful and energetic when free, and soft and quiet when handled. They should approach people in a happy friendly manner with eye-to-eye contact, keen and easy to train.

Size: *Standards:* 22 to 26 inches weighing between 25 kg and 40 kg; *Mediums:* 18 to 21 inches weighing between 15 kg to 25 kg; and *Miniatures:* 13 to 17 inches weighing between 10 to 20 kg.

Coat: Coat length should be 4 to 6 inches long. It should be straight, wavy or forming light loose spirals. It should not be too thick or dense nor should it be fluffy or fuzzy. It should be a single coat. Any sign of a double coat is a fault.

Hair: This is a temporary coat in the Australian Labradoodle and should be bred away from. This is a shedding coat and can shed in varying degrees and have several different looks ranging from sparse feathering on the legs and a bearded face to a shaggy all-over look. No matter the quantity of hair that is shed, a coat that sheds is considered a hair coat.

Fleece: This is a very soft coat that has close to the same texture as an angora goat. It is a non-shedding coat and can either have a straight wavy look or a soft spiraling curly look. This coat is an easy to manage coat and is highly prized.

Wool: This coat is reminiscent of a sheep's woolen texture. This is a non-shedding coat and can have a highly prized looser spiraling look which opens up easily to the skin, a tight dense curling look or a thick and very dense straighter look. It is recommended to breed away from the thick and dense wool coat as they are very high-maintenance compared to the looser spiraling wool.

Body: Height to length ratio should be 10 to 12 (being slightly longer in leg than body) but still appearing compact. Shoulders should have good angulation with firm elbows. Upright shoulders are a fault. Hindquarters should be of medium angulation with short strong hocks. Movement when trotting should be strong, with good reach and drive, giving the appearance of "going somewhere." When relaxed or at play they will prance and skim the ground lightly. Topline should remain level with strong loin and croup. They are a galloping dog; therefore flanks should rise up from a deep brisket, and well-sprung ribs.

Tail: Is preferred low set and saber like, a high set "gay tail" is permissible. Possum type or teapot handle tails are a fault. Padded, heavy or coarse appearance is a fault.

Head: Broad, well-defined eyebrows, medium stop, eyes set well apart, nose to eye longer than eye to oculus. The head should be clean and chiseled. A long, narrow or blockhead is a fault.

Ears: Set flat against head and should be level with eye. Leather should be of medium thickness and not hang below lower lip line. Excessive hair in ear canal is undesirable.

Eyes: Slightly round, large and expressive. Protruding or sunken eyes are a fault. Watery or tearful eyes are a fault.

Teeth: Scissor bite. Under or over bite is a fault. Crowding teeth in Miniatures is a fault.

Nose: Large, square and fleshy.

Pigment: Black or Rose. Pigment should be strong. Black pigmented dogs must have dark brown eyes. Pink spots or patches on nose, lips, eye rims or pads are a fault. Dogs with Rose pigment can have golden hazel or brown eyes. Eye rims should be Rose as should nose, lips and pads. Pink spots or patches are a severe fault.

Color: *Chalk:* A white colored puppy but if put up against a white surface will not be an exact match but rather a chalk in color. Nose pigment to be Black or Rose.

Cream: A soft Creamy coloring obviously not Chalk. Golden-Cream is a cream puppy with Gold or Gold highlighted muzzle or ears and are registered as Cream. Apricot-Cream is a cream puppy with Apricot or Apricot highlighted muzzle or ears and are registered as Cream. Nose pigment to be Black or Rose.

Black: A solid black in color with no "silvering" around eyes, muzzle, or pads. Nose pigment to be Black.

Silver: This color is highly desirable if it has an even platinum effect on the whole body though darker silver is acceptable. Silvers are born Black and will usually show signs of going silver on their muzzle around their eyes or around the pads of their feet. A silver may take from 1 to 4 years to complete. Nose pigment to be Black.

Blue: The blue coloring should have the "oily blue" effect on the coat with Blue pigmented skin and will be born this color; this color unlike Silver and Café does not change over time. Nose pigment to match the skin pigmentation.

Chocolate: A solid rich chocolate in color. Nose pigment to match the coat color. *Note:* A rich dark chocolate color is most desirable with no variation or fading, though a lighter and/or fading chocolate is acceptable.

Café: This color has a pinkie mauve or lavendery coloring. Cafés are born Chocolate with signs of going Café on the muzzle, around the eyes or around the pads of their feet. Like the silver, this color can take 1 to 4 years to complete. Nose pigment to match the coat color. *Note:* A "lighter chocolate" coloring is *not* considered a true Café but rather a less than rich chocolate.

Gold: This color is a solid Yellowy-Gold in color on the entire body and ears, no fading or variation is acceptable. Nose pigment to be Black or Rose in color.

Apricot: This color should be the same color as the inside of an apricot fruit. There is the tendency with this color to have darker ears, back "saddle effect" and muzzle. The solid Apricot color is most desirable but the darker variation of color on the points is acceptable. Desired nose pigment to be Black with Rose as acceptable.

Caramel: This is to be a solid Caramel coloring with no variation or fading. Nose pigment to match the coat color.

Red: This is a solid color with no variation or fading either in an "orangey" red or "mahogany" or "burgundy" red color. Nose pigment to be Black.

The Australian Labradoodle should be solid in color with no white markings. A small white flash no larger than 2.5 cm by 2.5 cm on the chest, feet or tail is permissible.

Special Qualities: There should be no body odor or "shedding." It is acceptable to "change coats" once a year seasonally and from puppy to adult, also during hormonal changes in fertile bitches. This coat must not shed, but should be groomed out. It is important that the coat gives the impres-

How They're Bred

Few of the designer dogs are mixed hybrid to hybrid. Labradoodles, which have recently been recognized as a breed in Australia and are slowly being recognized as such in other parts of the world, are one of the few that go back up to 15 generations. Dogs are recognized as a breed if there are at least three generations of hybrid-to-hybrid breedings, producing standardized offspring with similar sizes and predictable characteristics.

Most designer dogs are created by pairing pure-bred dogs together to achieve hoped-for results. The offspring will surely inherit some qualities from each parent. One won't know for certain without raising the dog and experiencing his temperament or viewing him as an adult.

Doodle 'Dos

In both the traditional Poodle-Labrador cross (F₁ Labradoodle) and the multi-generational Australian Labradoodle, there exists a wide variety of coat types. In the F₁ Doodle, the coat can be longish and wavy, short and wiry or bountiful and fluffy. The Australian Labradoodle coat tends to be more woolly or curly, like that of a pure-bred Poodle. This Poodle-type coat does not shed as much as the other coat types and is sometimes described as the fleece coat. Both the wavy coat and the woolly coat have curls, a celebrated feature inherited from the Poodle; the wavy coat tends to have loose spiral curls and the woolly coat, tighter curls. Depending on the coat type, the grooming requirements vary. Woolly or fleece coats with tight curls require more grooming than the other types, as the coat grows continuously and needs trimming about every eight to ten weeks. Doodles should never be clippered, but rather scissored in a teddy-bear cut about 2½ inches all around. Some puppy coats tend to mat during the transitional phase (between 8 and 12 months), and these coats benefit from daily brushing.

F₁-generation Labradoodles, being half Labrador, usually shed more and require more regular brushing than woolly-coated Doodles, though they do not need to be groomed at a salon like their woolly and wavy brethren. Some F₁ dogs hardly shed at all.

sion of being a fleece or wool rather than dog hair. The Australian Labradoodle should also display intuition about their family members or handlers' current emotional state or needs. This ability to "know" is what has made this breed an excellent dog for service animals for individuals with special needs.

Temperament: Extremely clever, sociable and joyful. Easily trained. Quick to learn unusual or special tasks. Active, a little comical at times. Can attempt to outsmart their owners if undisciplined. Friendly though obviously loyal to own family. Non-aggressive.

Faults: Yappy, highly strung, dominance/aggression, fearful/timid, aggressive to other animals. Special attention must be directed to soundness. It is the responsibility of conscientious breeders to test their dogs against HD, PRA, cardiomyopathy, elbow and patella disorders. It is good to keep in mind that the Australian Labradoodle has been bred as a family companion and service dog.

No one wants the heartache of illness and the expense of an ill dog.

There is no scientific laboratory proof that the Australian Labradoodle is hypoallergenic. Anecdotal research indicates that the fleece and wool textures of the Australian Labradoodle *are* very successful with asthma and allergy sufferers.

In these infant years of breeding the Australian Labradoodle, many first cross (F_1) and throwbacks will occur, with a wiry, sparse or half and half shedding type coat. These dogs need not be discarded for breeding, but can be assessed on their soundness of body and temperament. Many of these individuals offer valuable hybrid genetics and will breed on to an excellent Australian Labradoodle. In order to produce a breed of quality, haste should be made slowly. Genetic resources must be kept broad to protect the Australian Labradoodle breed from the disasters that many other breeds are suffering, "the genetic dead end."

Ask any qualified Labradoodle breeder:

Selecting a Labradoodle Puppy

The perfect family Labradoodle is outgoing and happy-go-lucky. This is an intelligent and bubbly dog. He's a dog that willingly comes to you but doesn't overwhelm you by jumping about, nipping or barking. The Labradoodle should be allergy-friendly, as the desirable coat types either do not shed or shed very little.

A pup with good conformation is of a type similar to a Labrador Retriever, only a little lighter and slightly longer than tall, whereas a Lab is more squarely built. The Labradoodle pup will have a saber tail, square head and moderate stop (point where the forehead meets the foreface). The head is very "Labby" in type, although not as heavy. A long Poodle-type nose should be avoided. The ear leather should be of medium thickness and the ear tips should not hang down past the jaw line. Again, "Labby" ears, but not as heavy. The pup's nose should be big and square.

The Labradoodle is considered a "trotting breed" like the Poodle, meaning that he should appear as though floating through the air when moving. A plodding pup does not have a desirable gait.

The price of a well-bred Labradoodle varies according to the dog's conformation, color and desired traits. A breeding-quality dog can run anywhere from $6,000 to $15,000, with the females being on the higher end. A pet dog can run anywhere from $700 to $2,500, plus shipping costs if you don't live near the breeder. That being said, the

"priceless" is just a pretty word.

RECOGNIZING A KNOWLEDGEABLE BREEDER

Ever walk into a kennel and want to hold your nose? Or walk into someone's back yard where there are "dog piles" everywhere or rusty old dog runs filled with puppies playing in their own messes? As much as you feel sorry for these puppies, you can be certain that they have not been bred by a knowledgeable breeder. This is not a breeder who should be getting designer-dog prices for his poorly bred and raised puppies. Moreover, these conditions should be reported to the appropriate authorities for the sake of the resident pups' (and their parents') welfare.

A knowledgeable breeder will maintain a clean, healthy environment for all dogs and puppies. The puppies will be socialized from an early age, receiving the attention and handling they need from the breeder. The puppies will also have received appropriate worming treatments and vaccinations prior to being allowed to leave the breeder's premises. A responsible breeder will also make sure that his puppies go to good homes. Be ready to be scrutinized prior to being allowed to purchase a pup.

national Labradoodle associations do not have long lists of accredited breeders. At the time of this writing, the Labradoodle Association of Australia listed 13 in Australia, 3 in Canada and 14 in the United States. The International Labradoodle Association also lists their accredited member breeders at www.ilainc.com.

Why choose a pup from an accredited breeder? The benefits are many. First of all, your breeder will be producing dogs that have good conformation and overall health. These breeders must sign a code of ethics, which obliges them to uphold strict standards in their breeding, puppy-rearing and puppy sales. Second, all of the breeding stock is registered, which means that records of the breedings and progeny are kept. Also, all accredited breeders must have their breeding stock DNA-tested. This further keeps track of bloodlines to continue stabilizing the breed and working toward recognition with the kennel clubs.

All puppies should be kept by the breeder until at least 10 weeks of age but are often kept longer, even up to 16 weeks of age so that they can have their hips and elbows checked and have their eyes tested for progressive retinal atrophy and entropion (an eyelid abnormality). Some breeders will do a heart check as well. As von Willebrand's disease is not common in the Australian lines, pups of Australian breeding are not checked for this, but pups in other countries may be. Von Willebrand's does exist in the Labrador Retriever and the Poodle, usually found only in poorly bred dogs. Nonetheless, it can be passed on to the puppies.

When visiting a breeder and litter, after looking over the conformation of the pups and checking that the litter and the parents have the necessary health clearances and documentation, the next step is temperament testing. There are several simple things you can do to assure that you take home the puppy that is most suitable for your family and lifestyle. After observing the litter, you probably have a pup that you are leaning toward. Perform these tests with the puppy that you are considering:

Friendly temperament, beauty and good health: the trio to strive for.

Test #1: Crouch low and walk backward, clapping your hands softly. Most Labradoodles will come running to you, as they are outgoing and friendly. If a pup doesn't respond in such a manner, that is not a pup you should consider.

Test #3: Drop something, such as your keys, a bone or a book. The Labradoodle pup should be curious about it. He shouldn't run away. He might even go up to it to check it out. A pup that runs away will not be a good choice.

Test #2: Touch the puppy all over. Take special care to touch his paws, ears and tail. If the pup allows this without trying to squirm away or put his mouth on you, he is a good candidate and you can proceed to the next test.

An easygoing Doodle puppy, smiling his way into someone's home.

Test #4: Roll your puppy over onto his back. Hold him there for a few seconds. After holding him there, rub his tummy. A good prospect will lie quietly, and if he gets a tummy rub for it, he'll quickly learn how to earn that reward. If the pup gets squirmy, gets mouthy or tries to get up, he will not be a good pup to put into a family with children.

Spend time getting to know all of the puppies in the litter.

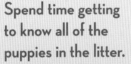

Once you have found a pup that passes all of the tests, and you've passed muster with the breeder, you are on your way to adding a new member to your family. Make sure that you are ready for this energetic, loving and loyal dog.

Test #5: Expose the pup to other animals such as other dogs, cats and other pets. Labradoodles tend to welcome other creatures of all types, rarely showing aggression or prey drive toward anything. However, this does not preclude their wanting to play with their new friends.

Veterinarians are meeting new Doodle puppies every day...

Caring For & Rearing the
Labradoodle
Pup

There's really not a whole lot of difference between raising a Labradoodle and raising any common breed of dog. As a household companion, he needs to be kept clean and given proper nutrition as well as to receive adequate healthcare, exercise, attention and education, just like any other dog!

PUPPY MEETS VET

The first thing that should be done upon getting your new Labradoodle puppy is a trip to your veterinarian. If this is your first pet and you don't already have a veterinarian, you should ask your breeder and other pet owners in your area for a recommendation. The little guy will need a thorough examination and a fecal test, and to be started on a series of vaccinations. Common vaccinations include parvovirus, influenza, leptospirosis, distemper, coronavirus and a preventive for kennel cough *(Bordetella)*. He should also be scheduled for his rabies vaccination, which is normally done at the age of four to five months.

Other things to consider are flea and tick preventives and a preventive for heartworm. There are many convenient ways to administer these to your pet, typically once a month, so ask your vet about the safest way to protect your Labradoodle. Another precautionary vaccination is the *Giardia* vaccine. Since your pup

aren't they the lucky ones?

will probably like to swim, there's a chance of his contracting an intestinal infection from the droppings of other animals who visited the same body of water. *Giardia* is a microscopic parasite that can cause diarrhea, vomiting and general discomfort. You'll need to discuss this with your pup's veterinarian.

Discuss the inoculation schedule for your Labradoodle with your veterinarian.

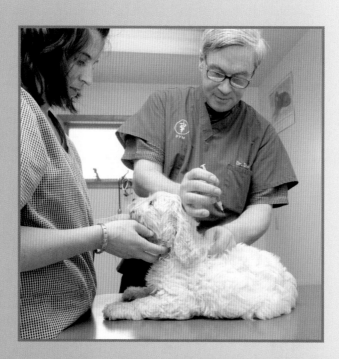

"You have no idea
how cold this table is!"

Unlike their Poodle forefathers, Labradoodles don't need expensive trips to the grooming salon. A once-a-week onceover is sufficient for a wavy-coated Doodle with this coat type.

GROOMING

Labradoodles are one of the easiest dogs to maintain. Their dense, curly coats repel both dirt and water. The desirable Labradoodle coat hardly sheds, if at all, and has natural lanolin in the coat similar to the Poodle ancestors. The lanolin keeps the dog's skin soft while repelling outside moisture. Many of the Labradoodle breeders in Australia bathe their dogs only once every six months.

The amount of time you spend brushing your dog depends on the type of coat. The fleece and woolly coats will need a thorough brushing only once a week, depending on the dog's habits. Fleece and woolly coats will require trimming a couple of times a year, depending on your preferences. Some woolly coats tend to be very thick and might require more frequent trimmings. The hair-type coat still sheds and will require more frequent grooming in order to keep the coat under control. However, due to this coat type's being more similar to that of the Lab's, you shouldn't have to trim the coat at any time.

As pups tend to get into dirty mischief, and Labradoodles do love water, you will have to clean your puppy (and adult) up from time to time before he comes back into the house. Of course he must be part of the family and welcome in your home! If the dog has been in the water, wait until he dries and brush him off. All dirt should come off with the brushing. If the dirt is dry already, simply brush it off. Like many other dogs, your Labradoodle may tend to roll in stinky things to hide his own scent, so you will also have to bathe your dog as needed. Try first to simply rinse your dog with water; if that doesn't work, you'll need to give him a full bath. Use a gentle shampoo formulated for dogs. A shampoo that is too harsh, including human shampoos, will remove the dog's natural lanolin, drying his skin and making his coat a dirt magnet. Should you have a Labradoodle that requires frequent bathing, Melinda Radus, the president of the Labradoodle Association of Australia, suggests using kelp, flaxseed oil and lamb bones to aid in the repair of a damaged coat.

Doodles love attention, especially from a young pal with a soft brush and gentle touch.

FEEDING

Many Labradoodle breeders are very conscientious about feeding their dogs a well-balanced, natural diet. Melinda Radus suggests the BARF diet (the Biologically Appropriate Raw Food developed by Dr. Ian Billinghurst), which includes raw meats and vegetables. You can purchase this type of diet at a feed store, have it delivered or make it yourself at home, as it consists of many of the foods you eat on a daily basis.

Generally, the meats are ground up but not cooked. Raw poultry is typically soaked overnight in grapefruit juice to eliminate any bacteria. Red meat should be thoroughly cleaned, as should all of the ingredients, including the vegetables and fruit. It's also good to add cooked rice and bran, as the dog requires roughage and fiber for solid stools. Bone meal is another additive that offers much-needed vitamins. The inclusion of omega fatty acids is also important, as it helps keep the coat soft.

However, it isn't necessary to feed a totally raw diet and you should not attempt raw-food feeding without researching the subject and getting advice from those with experience. Other options are to feed raw food in association with a commercial diet or to feed only a good-quality commercial diet. There are many commercially prepared dog foods that are of high quality. To figure out which dog foods really are quality foods, you will need to educate yourself. Don't just take advice and recommendations; read the labels!

Prior to buying a food, you'll want to know what the food contains. Ingredients are listed on the food package. The first three to five ingredients are the main constitution of the food. If you see anything with corn, wheat, by-products or rice hulls listed among the first five ingredients, steer clear. Read on and check for food colorings, preservatives and additives. Check the label for protein levels, as these are important when raising a fast-growing puppy. Some breeders suggest a

A DESIGNER DIET FOR ALL DOGS

Few dogs thrive on corn-based diets. You will rarely see a dog choose an ear of corn over a piece of meat. Dogs are carnivorous and therefore require the majority of their food to be meat-based. A quality dog food should contain meat as the main ingredient, and the remaining ingredients should include vegetables, brewer's yeast/rice, vitamins and omega fatty acids. Preservatives are not only a sign that rancid ingredients were used in the manufacturing of the food but can also be damaging, over time, to your dog's internal organs.

Veterinarians and breeders will normally steer their clients to either the brand they sell or have been using with their own dogs. Ask them why that particular food is one they recommend. What are the key nutrients? Why will this particular food give the dog a glowing coat and spring in his step?

The easiest means of choosing a food is to read the label. The first three ingredients are those that comprise the majority of the food. You should see actual meat within the first three ingredients, meaning beef, chicken, lamb or venison, not meal or corn or rice hulls. Actual meat. If you have a dog with beef allergies, try a fish- or venison-based diet.

Meat, it's what's for dinner!

Premium food for a premium Doodle, please.

protein level below 50% for both regular food and treats, as this will help the dog to grow at a more even pace instead of too rapidly, with the risk of developing growing pains, a condition in which the bones and muscles can't keep up with each other, causing lameness.

When using a commercial food, be sure to feed both canned and dry. The dry food, while good for the teeth and gums, is more processed than the canned food, meaning that it contains fewer vitamins. Canned food doesn't have to be processed as much, as the canning process helps to preserve the vitamins and moisture. Further, dogs don't get 100% of their moisture from drinking water. A good percentage of it comes from the foods they eat, which is another reason why it's a great idea to make canned food a part of your Labradoodle's total diet if you are feeding commercially prepared food. Not only will he receive better nutrition and more moisture, but the food will be more palatable to him and you can be sure that he will eat at his scheduled mealtimes (which also means more predictability with bathroom times).

Some owners prefer elevated bowls for their Standard Labradoodles, though there is still debate as to whether bowl stands are helpful or are actually harmful, increasing the risk of the dangerous bloat/gastric torsion. Discuss bloat with your vet.

Next to the Labradoodle, hydrogen and
oxygen form the best compound! When
your puppy is outside playing, offer him
fresh water to keep him hydrated.

Doodle to-go! Two
important components of
Labradoodle care are
exercise and grooming, and
this dog is enthusiastic
about both.

EXERCISE

Labradoodles can easily adjust to any living environment, provided they receive proper exercise. On-leash walks are good for both of you, but your Labradoodle also should have a daily free run in a fenced-in area. This can be in your fenced yard, but a Labradoodle will also enjoy romping with other dogs if there is an off-leash dog park nearby. Labradoodles need to socialize with other dogs on a regular basis. Social time aids in their own behavior as well as giving them the type of exercise that simply cannot be fulfilled by their human companions.

Should you live in an apartment and are away from home during work hours, you should try to find a doggie daycare center near you. Allow your Labradoodle to go to doggie daycare at least three times per week or even more frequently, if possible. This energetic, inquisitive and intelligent dog will not do well cooped up for long periods of time in a small space by himself. If you cannot locate a doggie daycare, then hire a dog walker or find a neighbor who is willing to spend a few hours with your dog each day. Who could resist a Labradoodle? Certainly not anyone who meets him!

Another option if you own a Labradoodle and spend many hours away from home is to consider obtaining a second dog. This gives companionship and a small feeling of pack unity, which furthermore offers your dog a sense of security. With canine companionship, your Labradoodle will be more content at home.

If you live in a single-family home or townhome, you most likely have a yard of some type. Make sure that the yard is securely fenced. The fence should be at least 6 feet tall the entire way around. Labradoodles are very athletic, and if left alone in the yard for too long of if otherwise bored, they can easily climb or jump out of any fencing less than 6 feet high.

Think positive. Think clean house.

House-Training the
Labradoodle

House-training begins the moment you bring your Labradoodle home. Just as if you were dieting, it's not something you do for only a couple of days; rather, it's a lifestyle for quite a while. Until good habits are formed, you must be diligent and consistent; the same goes for you and your puppy! You will begin by keeping an eagle eye on your puppy at all times. As the knowledge and the routine become ingrained within your Labradoodle, the dog will increase his control and his communication abilities.

As with all dogs, care must be taken to establish a consistent schedule for your Labradoodle's feeding times and relief times. This is how dogs learn. They have spectacular inner clocks that regulate their physical functions. If your Labradoodle knows what time he's going to eat and go outside, he can learn to control his bodily functions far more quickly than without this knowledge. Think house-trained in less than a week versus house-trained in three months.

Due to your Labradoodle's sensitive nature, you'll want to avoid negative associations with any learning experience. Positive reinforcement and redirection are the key words to training success. Always show your dog how to perform correctly. Don't rely on punishment for incorrect responses. Improper behavior happens, for the most part, because you do not properly guide and reinforce your

Think crate.

Doodles are naturally communicative and live to please their owners.

puppy. In other words, it does not occur because your puppy is vindictive, hateful or stupid. Labradoodles can be emotional, but these other characteristics aren't in his repertoire. Behaviors occur because of your communication, or lack thereof.

Let's begin with some very basic communication skills: vocal tones and visual cues. Starting off with vocal tones, there are three distinct tones that have meaning to your dog: a high, happy, enthusiastic tone when praising; a demanding tone when giving a command; and a low, growly tone when correcting. Keeping your volume down maintains the meanings of the tones. Raising your voice confuses the communication, so never shout, scream or yell. Your Labradoodle can hear far better than you can! Your dog will not ignore you if you are consistent and clear. If he understands what is being said and knows that good things happen when he listens, then he will surely respond.

As for visual cues, at least 70% of canine communication occurs through visual, or body, language. Each part of the dog has many nuances. Since we don't have movable ears, a tail or the ability to eject scent when we wish, we'll have to rely on two basic positions: dominant and submissive. The dominant position is when you are standing or sitting upright. The submissive position is when you are crouched down or lying on the floor. When giving a command or corrective tone, the dominant position will relay your message more effectively. When greeting your dog, playing with him or releasing him from work, the submissive position is best.

Does this help with house-training? Yes, immensely. Let's put it all together.

Start by scheduling your dog's feeding times. Let's say you feed your Labradoodle pup at 6 a.m., 12 p.m. and 5 p.m. Put the food down and be sure to pick up any uneaten food after ten minutes. This teaches your pup to eat at allotted times, not throughout the day.

Just like what goes in must come out, what goes out must come back in! Here's a puppy who knows the potty routine.

"Accident? What accident?"
Mum's the word.

If your pup is over five months of age, stick to feeding him twice a day.

Now we schedule the relief times. Choose a specific relief spot. This can be either a spot in your yard or, if you don't have a yard, on the curbside (be prepared to clean up after him!). Then choose a specific exit from your home. Always exit with your Labradoodle through the same door and go to the same spot. The less variation, the faster your pup will learn and the sooner he'll be able to let you know when it is time to relieve himself.

Next, establish the words you will use to cue your pup. Be sure everyone in the household uses the same words. Some examples are "Potty," "Hurry up," "Outside," "Business," etc. There are also phrases you can use to cue your Labradoodle that you and he are on your way out the door for his relief time, such as "Let's go outside." This phrase, paired with your actions of going to the door, gives your pup a clear definition. The best way to ensure that your pup

Scheduling

Maintaining a schedule will help both you and your pup, as you'll both know when it's time to go to his relief area. Dogs thrive on knowing what is going to happen and when, especially if it is rewarding to him.

For a young pup, under the age of 4 months, you'll need to take him to his relief area every 60–90 minutes. As the pup gets older, every two to three hours will suffice. The amount of time between potty breaks depends on the dog's activity level. The more sedate the dog, the less he'll need to relieve himself. The more he plays, such as when family members come home from school or work, the more often you should take him to his relief area.

It might help to write down the times as a reminder to you.

learns his potty word is to consistently use it at times when you know he's going to relieve himself. Labradoodles are so intelligent that this concept will be easily understood by the second or third repetition.

Before you go outside with your pup, get a special treat to bring with you. This treat is reserved specifically for potty success. As soon as your Labradoodle has completed relieving himself in the proper place, give him praise and the reward. The treat doesn't always have to be food. Labradoodles love to play and receive attention. A game of fetch can be equally as rewarding, as can a belly rub. Regardless of the reward, you should always use very

Labradoodles are quick learners: this little guy is taking the lead.

enthusiastic praise whenever your pup relieves himself outside. This reinforces his actions in the correct place, making him desirous of performing the behavior another time.

If your Labradoodle is under four months of age, he will need to relieve himself very often. You will need to take your puppy outside after he wakes up from naps, within 15 minutes of eating and during play. Keep these times in mind. Feeding times are scheduled, so you'll know when to take him outside, but napping and play times are inconsistent (although your pup will eventually get into some routine with these as well). You'll need to be aware of what your pup is up to and react accordingly.

Potty on Command

Just as you teach commands for many desired behaviors, it's also very convenient to have your dog potty on command. This will save many frustrating outings, waiting in bad weather or anxious that you'll be late for work because Junior is taking his sweet time sniffing, playing and avoiding the reason he was brought to his relief area.

Begin by going outside with your pup first thing in the morning. At this time of day, it's a sure thing that he must go immediately. Say the potty word (such as "Go," "Hurry," "Business" or "Potty") over and over until he goes. The moment he goes, praise him. Give him a treat when he is finished.

Every time you take your pup to his relief area, say the word over and over until he relieves himself. Repeat the rewarding words and treats as before. Within a week, Junior will potty on command.

HERE'S A SAMPLE SCHEDULE TO GET YOU STARTED:

6 a.m. Take the puppy outside. Say his relief word over and over until he goes. As soon as he goes, praise him. If he needs to do more, hold off on the treat until he is completely finished. Female dogs tend to get their business finished more quickly than male dogs.

6:30 a.m. Feeding time. Make sure your dog finishes his meal within the time allotted. In other words, whether he has finished or not, pick up his food dish after ten minutes. Always leave fresh water available. Keep an eye on your pup. If he begins to sniff and circle, get him to his relief area as soon as possible. Even without these cues, take him to his area within 15 minutes. Remain with him and give him his potty word over and over until he goes. Praise and reward.

Between 6:30 a.m. and 12 p.m. If your Labradoodle is under 4 months of age, make sure you get him outside every 60–90 minutes. Also, you'll need to feed him three times per day until he is five months of age. This more frequent feeding will increase his need to relieve himself. Each time you take him outside, keep him out there until he goes. He should have to urinate. Most dogs defecate twice a day, but pups might need to do so three or four times per day. Be aware of your pup's habits, and be sure to get him to his relief area during these times.

12 p.m. For pups on a three-a-day feeding schedule, feed and let out 15 minutes later. Again, continue taking him out every 60–90 minutes, or every 2–3 hours if over 4 months old.

5 p.m. Feed and let out 15 minutes later.

7 p.m., 9 p.m. and 11 p.m. Go outside. Using the potty word, make certain he does his business and then is rewarded.

THE CRATE ADVANTAGE

Crate training can be extremely helpful during house-training, especially if you cannot watch your dog every minute. How realistic is it to expect to be able to observe your pup around the clock? Not very. Teaching him to remain in the crate when you cannot watch him has many benefits related to house-training and all-around safety.

CRATE BENEFITS

1 The crate helps teach your Labradoodle to control himself. It is instinctive for a dog to not relieve himself in his den.

2 The crate keeps your dog safe and out of trouble when you cannot be with him. He cannot wander around the house, making messes, chewing furniture and risking danger.

3 Due to its den-like atmosphere, the crate gives your dog comfort. Many people don't like the idea of putting their young dogs into crates. This is a very human attitude, as we dislike being confined. Dogs, however, if left alone, will search out places that are barely large enough to hold themselves. In the wild, dogs will always search out dens to bear their young or maintain their own safety. They like feeling something solid all around them. It gives them a sense of security. This instinct is still very strong in domestic dogs.

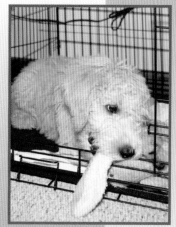

4 The crate is a place to which your dog can retreat when he is feeling overwhelmed or tired. If he doesn't wish to be in the middle of commotion or is tired, he will retreat to his safety zone.

Down time is den time, with a tasty chew.

Eager and happy to please, Labradoodle puppies make attentive students.

Begin crate training from day one. Put your pup's bed, food and water in the crate. Add several safe toys, especially interactive ones such as a food-filled bone or hollow rubber toy, soft squeaky toys and toys that both massage his gums and are edible. All these things make the crate an enticing room, much like one for your child. What child wouldn't want a room that has a comfortable bed and is loaded with toys and treats?

CRATE TIME

To teach your pup to go into his crate on command, do the following:

1 Sit near the crate and play with your pup.

2 Throw a toy or treat into the crate. Praise your Labradoodle as he retrieves the reward. Repeat this three to five times.

3 When your pup is comfortable moving in and out of the crate, briefly close the door. Remain sitting near the crate and continually praise him. Stick a treat through the openings so that your pup remains positive about the experience. Open the door and allow your pup to come out.

4 Gradually increase the time that your Labradoodle remains in the crate with you next to it. When he lies down and is comfortable, leave the room for a short period of time, about five minutes or so.

5 As long as your Labradoodle doesn't fuss, whine or scratch, return, give him a treat and open the door. If he does fuss, return and wait until he stops, then reward him and open the door. Try again. Repeat this process until your pup is comfortable.

6 Gradually increase the time that your pup is left alone in the crate. When he is quietly comfortable for upwards of half an hour, you can increase his crate time in half-hour increments. Within a week or less he should be able to be left for four to six hours.

Doodle puppy in toyland.

Doodle puppy in dreamland.

Every Doodle puppy starts out with
home schooling by mom.

When using the crate for house-training, you must be careful never to use it as punishment. The crate must remain a pleasant place for your Labradoodle. There is a way to use the crate to assure that your pup does his business when you wish. You don't want him to procrastinate or think that potty time is play time. If you have taken him out to potty and he does not do so within ten minutes, return inside and put him into his crate for half an hour. He can have his toys and soft bedding. He merely cannot have more freedom in the house at this point, as he may have to relieve himself.

Yes, this method is a means of "punishment" for not doing as you requested, but the pup doesn't know it! It is not a harsh punishment, and if the pup likes his crate, which he should, he won't think of it as punishment. The crate should never be used for "time-out" punishments. For example, you don't want to catch your pup chewing on one of your shoes, scold him and then put him into the crate. Using the crate in this manner would make it an undesirable place for your Labradoodle. The crate should be a safety zone, so always use a happy tone of voice when putting him in the crate.

RING BELL OR BARK FOR SERVICE

The next phase of house-training is to teach your Labradoodle how to let you know that he needs to relieve himself. Once he has a full understanding of where and when to do his business, he'll begin to control himself. As you increase the time between his elimination periods, your dog may have moments when he cannot stick to the schedule. A Labradoodle would be crestfallen to make a mistake. He must have some means of letting you know that he has to "go."

There are several ways for him to do this: he can bark and go to the door; he can scratch at the door; or you can teach him to ring a bell. The more subtle cues of sitting and looking at you or going to the door and waiting are typically ignored by us unobservant humans. Your Labradoodle is in the process of trying to figure out what will gain your attention. Be observant and reward the behaviors you are looking for. If your pup goes to the door, take him out. Should he go to the door and "speak," be sure to praise him as you take him outside, especially if he relieves himself. That earns a double reward, for both letting you know and going in the right place.

A very good means of communication is to teach your Labradoodle to ring a bell to let you know he needs to go out. This works not only when you're at home but also when you travel. Beware of one thing, though; he may ring it when he wishes to go outside to play.

There are two types of bells you can use: one that hangs from the doorknob or the desktop type commonly used at hotels and shops to garner attention. Each requires a different approach.

Hanging bell: Hang a small bell from the doorknob of the door you use to go out for potty trips. Each time you take your Labradoodle to the door to go outside, rub a small amount of cheese on the bell. Point it out to him, luring him to sniff it. As soon as he smells it, he will most surely lick it. When he makes the bell ring, take him directly outside and give him his potty word until he goes. Reward him again when he does his business. Repeat this every time you take him out. Within a week or less, he will connect the sound with going outside.

Desktop bell: Place the bell on the floor. Lure your pup to the bell using a treat. When he is close enough to touch the bell, praise him and give him the treat. Repeat this a few times until he becomes comfortable with the bell. Next, place a bit of the treat on the bell. Praise him when he takes it. Repeat this a few times. You can be sure he'll remain very close to the bell at this point. Next, you need to wait until he makes the move without your luring him. He'll go to sniff the bell to see if you "accidentally" dropped some treats that you haven't pointed out to him. When he does this, praise and reward him. At first he'll just look at you, wondering what he did to earn that reward. It will soon dawn on him to go check out the bell again; after all, it has yielded rewards in the past. When he does so, praise and reward him again. By this time you'll see the little light bulb over his head turn on. He will go to the bell and push at it with his nose. Again, praise and reward. The next time, however, make sure he makes the bell ring. No praise or reward until he does. As soon as he makes it ring, give him a treat and take him outside. Repeat this process each time you take him outside. With each successive session, he will make a more concentrated effort to ring the bell, and it will take him fewer tries. How much clearer can it be that your dog needs to go outside?

Any lesson can be mastered with a little encouragement and a generous helping of liver.

A happy family portrait is only a click away...

Obedience-Training the
Labradoodle

L abradoodles are extremely

sensitive creatures. They are also tremendously intelligent. It won't take more than one or two repetitions to teach any new behavior, provided the training is done in a positive, rewarding, clear and consistent manner. A Labradoodle does not learn well when force is applied. In fact, force can totally turn him off, often causing him to retreat into another room or his crate. If an exercise is broken down into small components, clearly defined and rewarded, a Labradoodle will quickly learn whatever you wish to teach him.

The best training approach is positive reinforcement. This is done with a reward, such as food, a toy or touch, and with something like the word "Good" or "Yes" to "mark" the moment that the dog does what you want him to do. You can also use a training tool called a clicker to mark the moment that your Labradoodle performs correctly. A clicker is a small rectangular box that makes a distinct noise when pressed. Regardless of the type of noise or word you use to mark the moment of a correct behavior, be consistent with it.

Before you begin, make a list of the things you wish to teach your Labradoodle. It's best to begin with the basic behaviors sit, stay, down and come. Once these four foundation actions are understood, you can build on them to accomplish whatever goals

positive reinforcement is the only way to go.

you set for your dog. It would also be a good idea to teach your Labradoodle how to walk on a loose leash, as this will be necessary for your everyday routine.

Begin by taking your dog into a quiet area where there are no distractions; this means no other animals, no toys and no extraneous noise. Labradoodles are highly perceptive of every little thing going on around them. Initially, you'll accomplish far more if you work in a quiet environment where your dog can concentrate on you instead of the distractions. If training outdoors, you will also want to make sure that the area is securely enclosed, no matter if working with your dog on- or off-leash.

We need to establish that the word "Good" or "Yes" (for our purposes here, I will use "Good") means that the dog is doing something well and will receive a reward for his behavior. If you are using another type of marker, such as a clicker or squeaker (yes, squeaky toys work well here,

too) be sure to pair the sound of the instrument with the moment your Labradoodle performs as you wish. Pairing the reward with the word "Good" and/or the sound of a click is a bridging signal. This means that the sound acts as a bridge between your dog's good behavior and his receiving his reward. Give your dog a treat as you use your bridging signal in order to teach him that the two are paired together.

The next exercise is called targeting. Your dog must learn to watch a specific object in order to earn his reward. The easiest object is your hand, as he'll need to learn specific hand cues for each exercise. Start by placing a piece of food in your hand and showing it to your Labradoodle. When he touches your hand with his nose, praise/click and give him his reward. Repeat this a couple of times until your dog is eagerly moving to your hand.

You can move your hand up and down and side to side. Each time you do this, require your dog to follow your hand with his nose. While he is doing

Your Labradoodle depends on you for guidance, understanding and affection.

so, praise him. When you finish the movement, give him a reward. Be sure he was able to follow your hand in all directions. Now that your Labradoodle knows how to target, you can teach him to come and sit.

Consistency...
the Key

If your dog learns what to expect and when it will occur, he will learn faster. Pairing specific vocal and language cues with a particular behavior will quickly teach your dog the meaning of your cues. The same cues will need to be used for a given behavior regardless of the situation. Changing the cues when there are distractions present will merely confuse your dog. Expecting less of your dog in the presence of distractions will also teach him that you don't wish for him to respond in certain situations.

Consistency, regardless of where you are and what is going on around you, will ensure clear communication and reliable, correct responses to your commands.

COME AND SIT

Begin by showing your dog the target to get his attention. Hold your hand in front of your knees. As he moves his nose toward your hand, go backward two steps. He will come toward you. When he does so, praise/click and give him his reward. The next time, take a few more steps backward, always luring your Labradoodle to come toward you.

After three or four repetitions, you should be going backward at least ten steps with your dog attentively coming toward you. At this time, add the word "Come" as you move backward. Your Labradoodle will soon associate the word with the action of coming toward you as he is rewarded for his response.

Next we add the sit command. This is also easily done through targeting. Simply place your hand (with the treat in it) over your dog's head and between his eyes. As he looks upward at his target, his rear end will lower. As soon as his rear end touches the floor,

LET'S TALK

Dogs understand that specific tones of voice have specific meanings. A high, happy and enthusiastic tone means happiness and/or pleasure. A demanding tone gives commands, while a low tone means anger or displeasure. You can use these tones of voice to teach your dog words. Use the high, happy tone when praising and using the words "Good" or "Yes." Use a low, scary tone when correcting your dog with "No," "Bad" or "Ahh, Ahh." When giving an instruction, be clear and commanding. As you give the command, be certain that your dog understands what you are saying by pairing it with an action. It often helps to lure the dog into the position you want as it makes the entire process more positive instead of coercive.

praise and give him his reward. After two repetitions, add the word "Sit" as you lure your dog into position.

Bring the two commands, come and sit, together for a chain of behaviors. This means that your dog has to perform more than one behavior prior to receiving the reward. This is how you can teach your dog to listen to you without giving him treats for every single thing he does. As he advances his knowledge and communication skills, he will be able to perform many commands before he receives any reward other than praise. Praise should never be withheld, as your Labradoodle thrives on hearing this from you.

Ready, SIT, Go!

"What's all this talk about heel? The toe smells good too."

HEEL

When your Labradoodle is very comfortable doing the come and sit, you can start teaching him to walk with you. For this exercise, the commands you will use are "Heel" and "Sit." This time, instead of moving your target backward with you, you will be moving it forward with you. Also, you'll be keeping your target at your side because that's where you want your dog to be while walking with you. This position prevents your tripping over him and helps him watch you better.

After doing a come and sit, put yourself at your dog's side. Which side doesn't matter, although most people will walk their dogs on their left side. If you wish to walk your Labradoodle on the left, be sure to use the visual cue of stepping out on your left leg first as you give the heel command. Should your dog walk on your right side, use your right leg first as you give the command. The idea behind this is that beginning with the leg closest to the dog is a stronger visual cue than having the opposite leg begin walking. The movement will encourage your dog to begin walking with you.

Since your Labradoodle is now familiar with following the target, you can begin using the command "Heel" on that very first step forward. Keep the target at about knee level, where your dog can easily see and smell the reward. Go forward two to five steps, stop and tell your dog to sit. If your target remained at your side, near your knee, your Labradoodle will also be there, sitting as you had requested. Be sure to praise/click and reward.

If your dog did not move with you, lure him with the treat. Don't go back to him; encourage him to come to you. Once he's at your side, go forward only two steps, stop, tell him to sit and reward him. Sometimes you need to progress a little more slowly.

When he's able to remain at your side for two to five steps, increase the amount of steps between each stop and sit. As Labradoodles are very quick and intelligent, it may take less than 5 minutes to build up to

20 steps. Once the two of you have accomplished 20 steps, incorporate turns and changes of pace. Always keep your target where your dog can see it, and give praise the entire time your dog is moving with you.

When your Labradoodle can walk with you and come readily, it is time to move your training sessions outdoors or, if you were already in a quiet area outdoors (fenced, of course), move to somewhere that presents minor distractions. The distractions can be as simple as a different surface, such as grass if you had been practicing on a tile floor, or things like dog toys that might capture your dog's interest. It's especially helpful if you can get someone to throw some dog toys around while you work with your dog. This helps with the overall distraction-proofing required to do any activity successfully with your Labradoodle. Up until this point, since you were in an enclosed space, you did not need to have your pup on leash. When you start introducing

Having a ball can be even better than just a treat. Balls last longer.

distractions would be a good point to introduce the leash, since the goal of this training is to have your Labradoodle walk on a loose leash.

If something causes your dog to turn his attention from you, you'll need to regress to a point in your training where he was more focused on you, and be more gradual in

introducing the distraction. Also, you may want to change the reward into something more valuable to the dog. For example, he sees a ball and wants very much to get the ball instead of watching your target. Obviously, the ball is more of a reward than the treat. Pick up the ball and use that to target him. After a few

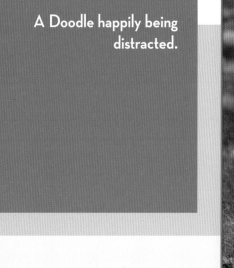

A Doodle happily being distracted.

heel/sit or come/sit repetitions, let him mouth and play with the ball. Then return to the exercises using his chosen reward.

When moving toward something that distracts your Labradoodle, the best way to regain his attention is to turn in the opposite direction. When he is back to watching you, have him sit and reward him. It may take a while to walk around the block, but your dog must learn to do so on a loose leash, not pulling you along. Many dogs are rewarded for just moving forward, so be sure that your Labradoodle receives his reward on a loose leash, not by pulling ahead.

Be clear in your commands and confident in your stature, and you'll both be smiling through obedience lessons.

SIT AND STAY

With the come, sit and heel exercises under your Labradoodle's collar, it's time to begin the stay exercise. This might be difficult for a young Labradoodle and more comfortable for a dog over one year of age. You see, puppies have a difficult time staying still for more than a few seconds, while an older dog prefers to remain still and observe his surroundings.

To build a solid stay, you need to break the exercise down into three components: time, movement and distance. Later, once all of these elements are accomplished, you can add distraction-proofing as well.

First we will discuss the time factor. This is added very gradually, beginning with only two seconds and aiming for the goal of one minute. Begin by working on the behaviors with which your dog is familiar—the heel, sit and come. Next, stop and have your dog sit at your side. Prior to giving him his reward, which signals the end of the exercise, put your hand in front of his face with your palm facing him and tell him to stay. If your dog is easily distracted, don't move yet. If he's comfortable with remaining still for a few seconds, step in front of him using the opposite leg of the one you use to start the heel command.

If working with a pup under six months of age or with an insecure dog, go ahead and target your dog as he remains in the sit/stay. The target should be held steadily, just above his nose, so that your dog doesn't move. As he remains in place, praise him. Return back to the heel position and reward him as you continue to praise. This first attempt should not last more than a few seconds at best. You want to set up your Labradoodle for success, not failure, so be certain to begin at a point where your dog is successful and build from there.

While your dog is remaining in place, be sure to praise him. Don't get super-giddy in the praise, just be enthusiastic that your dog is performing. Labradoodles love to be praised, but if you get him too excited, he won't be able to

remain in the stay position. You might need to tone it down just a bit.

The next time you attempt the stay, add a few more seconds before returning to the heel position and rewarding your dog. Sometimes it's difficult to know exactly how long you are maintaining the stay. I usually count by how many times I say "Good dog" (or "Good girl," "Good boy," etc.). It takes about a second to say this, and as your dog gets better at the stay command, you just keep adding "Good dogs." Eventually, after about 20 "Good dogs," it becomes more of a tongue-twister than a form of praise, so you can tone it down to a "Good dog" every couple of seconds.

There might be times that your Labradoodle will attempt to get out of remaining in place. This will happen more and more often if you don't acknowledge his behavioral thresholds. A behavioral threshold is the period of time for which your dog can maintain a specific behavior. If he moves out of position, it means his threshold has been breached. You've attempted to make him remain in place for longer than he is able to at that time. Should this happen, back up to the length of time at which your dog was successful. For example, at around 20 seconds your dog moves out of his stay position. However, during the previous attempt at 15 seconds, he remained in place.

Should a behavioral threshold be breached, you will need to regress a bit in order to go back to progressing. Using the aforementioned example, go back to the 15-second time

One member of the family should be in charge of the Labradoodle's lessons but all should help reinforce what he's learned.

span and work at this level for a few sessions. Reward your dog as he works hard and does as you command. When he has performed consistently at this level, gradually move on to the next. If a five-second increment was too much, do a two- or three-second increase.

If your dog moves out of position for any reason, always return him to the position in which you had originally placed him before starting again. You can either lure him there with your target (which is the easiest way unless he's distracted) or you can guide him there with the use of a leash. Once he's back in place, reiterate the stay command and return to his level of success. Labradoodles are very quick, but sometimes they can be easily intimidated or flustered. Take your time and implement your training in a methodic and positive manner. This will ensure that your dog fully understands the exercise at a given level prior to proceeding to the next one.

Once you've accomplished adding time to the exercise, you can begin to incorporate the next factor, movement. You will begin by moving around your dog, still remaining close enough to touch him, from standing in front of him to moving along his sides to eventually walking all the way around him.

Begin by stepping side to side in front of him. Keep your leash loose and, if your dog has a tendency to scoot in your direction, keep the target directly over his nose. As he learns to remain still while you move, you can gradually hold the target farther away; do this by moving your hand only, not your whole body. While you step from side to side, remain close enough to touch your Labradoodle on the head. A common error at this point is to move backward as you do the side-stepping. This is rushing ahead to where you are setting up your Labradoodle for failure. Remember, you want to set him up for success. Take it one step at a time.

When your dog has maintained his sit/stay during the side-to-side movement, begin to move along both of his

Keep lessons short and fun. Doodles bore quickly.

sides. Begin with going to his shoulder on each side. As he becomes comfortable with that motion, go toward his hip on each side. It's okay for your dog to move his head to watch you and his tail to express himself, but he can't scoot his rump around to keep an eye on you. Should he do so, replace him in the same spot and reiterate the stay command, complete with your hand signal and body position as a visual cue.

The next step is to move completely around your Labradoodle. As your dog targets on your hand, keep your hand still as you walk around your dog. This is similar to placing your hand on a bat held vertically and walking around the bat while keeping it standing, except that you will not be touching the dog. If you move your hand, you move the dog. Keep your hand still and your dog remains still. Should your Labradoodle be at the point where he doesn't require direct targeting, keep your hands above your waist as you move around him. Always praise enthusiastically as he remains still.

After accomplishing one time around, go for two, then three and so on. Be sure to move around in both directions or you'll get dizzy and your dog will learn to only accept your movement in one direction. Change your direction and teach your Labradoodle to accept any movement around him.

If using a clicker to bridge the stay, click when the stay exercise is complete, not during the exercise. You will, however, use praise during the exercise. The click signifies the end of an exercise, telling the dog that he's about to receive his reward. However, as your dog progresses, you can use the click to signify the end of a specific behavior during a behavior chain. But we are getting ahead of ourselves; that's more advanced training.

When your dog is comfortable with your movement, he'll learn to be comfortable with

Naturally Labradoodles go to the head of the class. Obedience school can be terrific for owners and dogs alike.

your increasing your distance (the third factor) as you move around him. You will spiral out, gradually increasing your distance with each successive stay command. Begin with a stay in which you move around your Labradoodle in both directions. Make sure he's comfortable with your movement and with the amount of time he must remain in position. You must also make sure that you no longer have to do direct targeting as you move around him. If you must still do this, he's not ready for you to increase your distance.

Should your Labradoodle be fully comfortable without seeing his reward, go out about a foot away from him as you move around him. Always keep your eyes on him, praising him as he remains in place. As your Labradoodle learns to accept a distance of one foot away, go for two feet. Each successive time you have him do the sit/stay, add another foot of distance until you are at the end of your leash. Please take note, however, that you should begin training with a 5- or 6-foot leash, not a 20-foot leash. That would be expecting far too much from a beginner. If you are doing this off-leash and indoors, don't go so far away that you can't readily replace your Labradoodle into his spot if he should get up.

There are so many uses for the stay command. You can teach your Labradoodle to stay at the door or to remain in place while being examined or bathed, and the stay exercise forms the basis of many more behaviors and tricks. Once this word is understood, the sky's the limit.

Practice every command once or twice before taking a break or moving on to the next one.

DOWN AND STAY

The difficult part of this exercise is teaching your Labradoodle to assume the down position on command. Once he's down, the stay will be easy, as he already knows its meaning. He must simply transfer it from the sit position. This is an easy association for the intelligent and willing Labradoodle.

You must make the down exercise pleasant for your dog, as the down position is a submissive one. For some dogs, it's tough for them to assume a submissive position on command. This is not necessarily so with Labradoodles, but there are always exceptions.

The first method you should use is to bait him into position. There are two ways you can do this, from either the heel position or from in front of your dog. You'll probably be more successful standing in the heel position (next to your dog), for you can easily guide your Labradoodle into the down position should he resist. If you are standing in front of him, you won't be in a convenient position. However, a young pup might easily follow the bait down, and you won't have any issues to contend with.

As with everything, you may encounter a few trouble spots. Your dog might not be willing to go all the way into the down position. He may follow the treat with his nose and upper body, but his rear end remains up. Or he may move around, trying to obtain the reward without putting any part of himself down. The reasons for this vary: he may not like the surface you have chosen for this exercise; he simply may not be willing to put himself into the down position or it may be another reason altogether.

The way you handle this depends on whether you have the time to be very patient or you need him to learn the behavior immediately. There are always scenarios in which you'll want to achieve this quickly; for example, you are sitting at the table and eating, and you want your dog to appear less formidable to a child or you want him not to

CLICK AND TREAT

Be ready to use lots of treats when clicker training. Dogs of all breeds and mixes will work for rewards. Clicker training has gained popularity as a positive-motivational-training method and can be used on any living creature from fish to dog to horse to elephant.

Essentially, the sound of a clicker marks the moment that the animal has performed the correct behavior. As the animal learns that the sound of the click means he'll be receiving a reward, he'll strive to earn the click. If confused, he might perform some random behaviors in the hope of earning the click and subsequent reward.

Those using clicker training should carefully observe their pets and practice moving their thumb prior to actually using the clicker. Timing is everything.

jump up on an elderly parent. In any case where you need quick results, you'll need to do the following to achieve an expedient down:

Give your Labradoodle the down command, using the lure. As he follows the lure in one hand, apply gentle pressure just behind his shoulder blades with the other. He should easily complete the down movement. As soon as he does so, praise and give him his reward. Also, release the shoulder pressure and let him up again. I do suggest, however, that you don't just let him get up and go on his way. Take him into a forward heel exercise so that his movement remains your idea, under your control.

If you have more time and you are opting for the method that requires no placement or coercion, you'll need to use behavior capturing and shaping. This requires a timely acknowledgment of when your Labradoodle does something that you want him to do, as

Hands can give commands.

HAND SIGN LANGUAGE

Just as those with hearing disabilities use sign language to communicate, you can do the same with your dog. As you speak human and Fido speaks canine, the use of hand signals helps bridge the language barrier.

You can use your hand first as a lure, with food, and then as a signal all its own after the dog learns the meaning of each particular gesture.

well as loads of patience. This method, commonly used with clicker training, rewards the dog for "throwing out" behaviors. This means that your dog will constantly be trying things to gain your recognition and rewards. It teaches the dog to think, which means loads of stimulation. The only problem is that it's tough to shut it off when you wish, without doing a specific requested behavior such as stay.

To accomplish the down command using behavior capturing, you'll need to stand by and observe your dog. Always have his reward handy, for the moment may come quickly and you must be timely in delivering the reward. You are watching for your dog to lie down. As soon as he does, you'll click/praise and give him his reward. He may stand around a few minutes, wondering what he did to receive that reward. He'll throw out other behaviors to see if they work. Don't give in. Wait

By using the lure, the dog will learn the meaning of the gesture. Within a short time, the gesture alone is all that is needed, while your praise and a treat are rewards for a proper response. Your legs, shoulders and facial expressions can also be utilized to communicate. Dogs are very aware of our most subtle body movements.

Now we're talking!

Hands can give cookies.

for him to lie down again.

After three to five repetitions, your Labradoodle will understand. You'll see that light bulb over his head turn on as he starts lying down in front of you every chance he gets. Once that light bulb is activated, add the verbal command "Down" to his action. It will take a few more repetitions for the dog to associate the word with the action.

You might need to have your Labradoodle do a few different exercises between the down commands. This way, he won't just lie there waiting to be rewarded. He learns that the actual action of lying down is what earns him his reward.

Whichever method you choose to teach the down, once your dog has an understanding of the exercise, it's time to teach him to stay in that position. It won't be difficult, as he's already familiar with the stay command. Before giving him the stay command, make certain he's comfortable in the down position. He should be relaxed and not pushing against your hand or

scrambling to get up.

If he isn't relaxed, try rubbing his ears, chest or tummy. Use slow, calming strokes as you praise him. Not too many dogs will pass up a tummy rub. I'm sure he'll be relaxing into position in no time. You might even find that when he approaches you for attention, he drops to the floor and shows you his tummy, ready for a rub!

Remember not to do the down several times in succession, as that teaches your Labradoodle a pattern instead of attentiveness and obedience. Vary the exercises and keep him guessing what you'll be doing or requesting next.

Gradually increase the stay time with each successive down command. When you begin your movement, instead of stepping in front of him, as you did with the sit/stay, you should first step behind him. If he shows any signs of insecurity, you'll need to bend over and caress him as you move. This is not easy, but it is necessary for continued positive training in an instinctively uncomfortable position.

Once your Labradoodle is comfortable with your stepping behind him during a down/stay, go to his other side. Continually praise him, petting him if necessary. With each successive down/stay exercise, increase your movement around him. In a very short time you should be able to move entirely around him. If you've been touching him, gradually decrease the amount of touch as you practice the down/stay exercise. A light touch on his head or side should suffice for a while.

As your dog gains confidence with your movement while he remains in the down/stay, begin gaining a bit of distance. Do this very gradually, as you did with the sit/stay. With each successive stay command, step out a foot or so as you walk around him. In the same training session during which you began moving around your Labradoodle during a down/stay, you should be able to walk around him at the end of your 6-foot leash.

Doodles dawdling and diddling: even smart dogs will be dogs.

Every time you say "Come," your Labradoodle should expect good things.

Born retrievers, Labradoodles love any game that involves something to chase.

COME FROM STAY

Now that your Labradoodle can do both the sit/stay and down/stay, you can call him to come to you from either position as well as from anything else he may be doing. You'll need to practice the exercise from different places around him, ensuring that he will come regardless of where you are and what he is doing.

One thing of which you should be aware is anticipation. It's very easy to pattern-train a Labradoodle. You need only have him perform a chain of behaviors two times in succession. A typical behavior chain is to do a sit/stay, then take a few steps back and do a come. Try not to fall into this pattern, as it will extinguish your dog's ability to remain in the stay position. He'll already anticipate that the second you begin to move away from him, he's to get up and come to you.

Vary the exercises enough to avoid pattern-training. Alternate at variable intervals between the come from stay and returning to heel position, or even releasing him from work after a stay exercise. Keep him guessing and therefore attentive.

Also, never go straight out away from your dog prior to doing a come, and especially never walk straight back from him when either doing a come from a stay or just moving away from your Labradoodle during a stay. Your "walking backward" movement is signaling to your dog that you are about to call him to come, since that's how you taught him to come in the first place. He'll get up before you even give the command, for he has already learned the visual cue.

Try putting your Labradoodle in a stay and walking around him, gradually increasing the distance. As you walk, take out a reward, hiding it a bit so that your dog won't get anxious. Somewhere along the way, turn and face your dog and call him to come. As you call him, bend forward at the waist to look more inviting. "Reel in" (without pulling) the leash as he comes. Praise him the entire time he is coming to you. This will encourage him as it rewards his actions. Hold the treat where he can see it, about hip height, and as he comes in to you, stand upright. When he arrives, tell him to sit. After he sits, he receives his reward.

You'll have to do a bit of distraction-proofing by "faking him out" every so often. Sometimes, as you move around him, stop and face him but don't call him to come. If he remains in place, reward him with praise, return to him and give him the treat. Then, again tell him to "Stay" and move around him.

You have now completed some basic commands. By no means should you be satisfied with simply imparting this bit of knowledge. There is so much more for your Labradoodle to learn and so many things you can do with him. These are just the basics. Your dog is capable of incredible things. Read on to discover some of the activities available for you and your Labradoodle.

Enjoy your Labradoodle lakeside...

Experience Labradoodle *Fun*

Your Labradoodle can partake in nearly any activity you wish, although he will not be able to participate in certain events sanctioned by kennel clubs that don't recognize mixed breeds. His potential ranges from the helpful to the competitive to the just plain fun! Let's begin by discussing the reason Labradoodles were developed—to be assistance dogs.

Labradoodles are intelligent, versatile and able-bodied. They also come in non-allergenic varieties. This allows those who are both physically disabled and suffering from allergic reactions to dog dander to have the canine assistants they so badly need, aiding them in their goal of independence. An assistance dog is normally raised in a foster home where he is socialized and obedience-trained. Upon reaching maturity he is taken to a training school where he will learn how to help the disabled. This training can take up to a year or longer. When the dog is fully trained, his human partner is brought in, and they spend several weeks together, learning how to communicate with each other as well as how to become compatible. When the Labradoodle "graduates" to his job and new life, he can be upward of two years old. It's a long process that starts in puppyhood, but one enjoyed immensely by this magnificent dog and all who work with him. Labradoodles love the challenges presented and the attention. Nothing is better for them than to have a daily job and someone who adores them.

he'll bring you sticks, birds and joy!

COMPETITIVE SPORTS

Labradoodles excel in obedience, agility, flyball and many other activities. However, due to the breed's not being recognized by the American Kennel Club, they can only attend training, practice and fun matches held by the AKC. Similar rules apply in matches as in sanctioned trials, but no certificates of accomplishment are issued. There are some trials held by dog clubs that allow all dogs to compete, regardless of breed. In these cases, there may be club certificates and rewards. One such club is the United Kennel Club (UKC), a national club in the US. While they do have a registry for pure-bred dogs, they allow dogs of all breeds to compete in performance events. You likely will also find a local or regional "all-breed" or "all-dog" club with no restrictions on the dogs that can compete, or you may find a local kennel club that allows your Labradoodle in matches.

Obedience trials typically encompass three levels of competition: Novice, Open and Utility. Once these levels are completed, you and your dog can strive for obedience trial championships. Following are explanations of some of the exercises that are generally found at each level of competition, although these can vary depending on the club hosting the competition.

At the Novice level, the dog and handler usually complete two separate sets of exercises. In the first set, only the handler and dog are in the ring. The judge calls out exercises and the dog-and-handler team executes them. The exercises include heeling both on and off leash, performing a figure-8 on leash while heeling, remaining in a stand/stay while the judge walks around and touches the dog and performing a sit/stay then recall (come) from 30 feet away. A finish is also requested. The finish is an exercise in which the handler tells the dog to put himself into the heel position. The dog then places himself at his handler's left side, either by going behind the handler or by swinging around in front of the handler. The method the dog uses to attain this objective depends largely on the dog, as dogs tend to have a preferred direction. This is usually discovered by the handler early in the training process so that there aren't any "surprises" in the competition ring.

The second set of exercises consists of group stays. In the Novice level, the dogs are lined up on one side of the ring, side by side, approximately 2 feet away from each other. There are never more than 12 dogs in the ring. As a group, the owners must face the opposite end of the ring with their dogs sitting in the heel position. At the judge's command, the handlers tell the dogs to stay, walk to the other side of the ring and turn to face their dogs. The dogs must remain in the sit/stay for a complete minute, whereupon the judge tells the handlers to return to their dogs. If a dog breaks his position anytime throughout this exercise, he will be disqualified from the class. This exercise is repeated in a down/stay, which lasts for three minutes.

The next level, Open, has similar exercises, yet everything must be performed off leash. One of the different exercises is the drop on recall. This means that the dog is told to stay at one end of the ring while his handler goes to the other end. The judge signals the handler to do a recall (come). When the dog is halfway to the handler, the handler signals the dog to lie down. Once the dog is down, the judge signals the handler to complete the recall. Once the dog is sitting in front of the handler, the judge signals for the finish. And all of that is just for the drop on recall exercise!

Another exercise is the retrieve on the flat. The dog is told to stay and the handler throws a dumbbell at least 20 feet in front of the team. The judge signals the handler to send the dog. The dog then must retrieve the dumbbell and come back to sit in front of the handler. The dog holds the dumbbell until the judge signals the handler to take it, upon which the dog drops the dumbbell into the handler's hand. The finish is also required to complete the exercise.

The final exercise in Open is the broad jump. The criteria for this exercise depend upon the rules of the hosting club. Some clubs require the handler to stand at the side of the jump as the dog goes over the jump, sits in front of the handler and then returns to heel position. Other clubs allow the handler to be on the other side of the jump, facing the dog prior to issuing the command; the dog then sits in front of the handler after completing the jump.

The Open group exercises are similar to the Novice and differ only in that the dogs must remain in a sit/stay for three minutes and a down/stay for five minutes with the handlers out of sight. This requires some heavy-duty distraction-proofing, as there are hundreds of dogs and people at shows, and the dogs in the ring must have faith that their handlers will return.

Once a dog has accomplished the Novice and Open classes, he can go on to the

Be your Doodle's biggest fan! Knowing they're pleasing their owners, Labradoodles can reach any height in obedience.

Utility level. When exhibiting a dog in obedience classes, you must go through them in order of difficulty. However, this does not mean that you need to teach your Labradoodle only the exercises he needs to know for the level at which he's participating. In fact, your dog will be more willing to execute all of his commands if you keep him stimulated, and that is accomplished through always teaching him new behaviors. Your Labradoodle can have an understanding of all the exercises of the Utility level and beyond even though he's only performing in the Novice class.

Utility is quite a class to observe, as many of the cues are delivered visually. The first exercise is the heel, using only visual cues. Upon near-completion of the heeling exercise, the dog is left in a stand/stay with the handler walking forward another 20 feet and stopping. Upon the judge's signal, the handler calls the dog to the heel position, using a visual cue. The remaining exercises include scent discrimination, object discrimination and directed jumping.

In scent discrimination, the dog must retrieve both a leather and a metal object containing the handler's scent. There are 11 other identical objects in the same location without the owner's recent scent. In object discrimination, the dog must retrieve a glove from a specific location. There are three identical gloves laid out in a line. The judge tells the handler which glove to have the dog retrieve and the handler then signals the dog to execute it. The dog returns with the glove, sits before the handler, drops the glove upon command and completes the exercise with a finish.

There are several parts to directed jumping. The first is the "go out," in which the dog must go away from the handler to the opposite side of the ring, turn and sit to face the handler. There are two jumps in the ring, parallel to each other, yet at least 10 feet apart. One is a bar jump and the other a flat-panel high jump. The judge tells the handler which jump he is to have the dog go over. The

Keeping Busy

Organized activities aren't the only things you can do with your dog. There's hiking, biking, swimming, hunting and more. Labradoodles love to run and swim, and don't forget their doubled-up sporting-dog blood. They not only have the Labrador Retriever in their background but some lines also carry Irish Water Spaniel and Curly-Coated Retriever blood. And, as history shows, the Poodle was a prized hunting dog throughout Europe. With some training, Labradoodles will flush out game, point to its location and retrieve it from any type of cover or water. They have a keen eye, great memory and versatility and truly are wonderful all-around companions for whatever you like to do!

handler relays this message to the dog, who then jumps and returns to the handler, sitting nicely in front of him. The judge then signals for the handler to have the dog finish. This is repeated with the other jump.

An exercise at all levels of UKC obedience is the honoring exercise, in which a dog remains in the down position in a designated area of the ring while another dog is working through the exercises. The honoring exercise is evaluated on how well the dog responds to his owner's down command, how he reacts (or does not react) to his handler's moving away from him and how he behaves while the other dog is working.

Regardless of whether or not you wish to exhibit your Labradoodle in obedience shows, these are some great ideas for teaching him new behaviors. There are many ways you can set up your own jumps, such as a board placed between two trees or two chairs. You can do the figure-8 around cones or bushes. You can obtain three gloves and teach him the directed retrieve. The possibilities are boundless.

This brings us to agility. Talk about opportunities to learn and have fun with your Labradoodle! Just going to agility class is loads of fun; there is no need to compete. Then again, if competition is your goal, there are many ways to do this other than an AKC-sanctioned trial.

Family time with the Doodle. It doesn't get better than this.

There are several levels of agility, but the fun is in the learning. There are A-frames, seesaws, different jumps, a dog-walk, tunnels, weave poles, crawl tubes and much more. It's more than just teaching the dog to negotiate the obstacles, as you also must learn how to move around the course while guiding your dog correctly. This sport requires fast thinking and fast motion. You can be certain that your Labradoodle will love it.

Flyball is another great sport. Although still in its infancy, you should be able to find a training club in your area that offers this fun relay race. In a flyball race, there are normally four teams of four dogs and handlers each. Teams stand at one end and release their dogs to run down a lane (which has four jumps for the more advanced teams) and stomp on a board at the end of the lane, which releases a tennis ball. The dog must catch the ball, run back to his handler and hand over the ball. Once the dog returns, the next dog is released. The first team to have all four dogs go through the course wins the race.

Another timed event is rally obedience (or "rally-o"). This has recently become very popular. It is similar to obedience competition, only it is timed. There are more types of heeling exercises (than in the obedience ring), involving spiraling and turning in different directions. It's much like a dance, only each exercise has a number and must be done

in order. As a fast-moving, ever-changing activity where the dog can be encouraged throughout, Labradoodles will excel.

Speaking of dance, another great sport to recently reach popularity is freestyle. This is essentially "dancing with dogs," and freestyle events are open to all types of dogs. There are judged events throughout the world, with the World Wide Freestyle Association leading the way. This activity involves using one's imagination to create routines from your dog's natural and trained behaviors. Set to music, a single exhibitor with one or more dogs, or a team of exhibitors and dogs, performs a choreographed routine. Usually the exhibitors wear some type of costume, with the dogs wearing something to match!

Life with the Labradoodle is action-packed. Enjoy every moment of every day with your Doodle.

INDEX